Energy Boundaries

How to Protect & Affirm Your Personal Space

Volume 1

Brian D. Parsons

Samarpan Alchemy Publications

Energy Boundaries: How to Protect & Affirm Your Personal Energies - Volume 1

ISBN 978-1-907167-10-2

Published by:

Samarpan Alchemy Publishing
P.O. Box 813
Exeter
EX5 4WF
United Kingdom

Email: info@samarpan-alchemy.co.uk
Web: www.samarpan-alchemy.co.uk

Dedicated to:

My Mother and Father

With love, for everything

May God go with you through all the dark places you must walk.

An ancient Egyptian blessing

Contents

Medical & Psychiatric Disclaimer:

The information contained in this book is aimed at resolving emotional, mental and spiritual issues, and is not intended to directly resolve physical and / or medical complaints and illnesses.

In all such cases, individuals are strongly advised to consult with a qualified medical practitioner about their physical condition.

If an individual is suffering from severe emotional and / or mental conditions, it is also strongly advised that they consult a qualified medical practitioner or other qualified mental health specialist.

Individuals should only use the information contained in this book in accordance with the laws and regulations of their country of residence.

Audio Essences, Crystal Holograms & Energy Cards:

In addition to crystal layouts, this book includes three additional ways to work with the techniques and processes contained within, namely:

- Audio Essences
- Crystal Holograms
- Energy Cards

More information on each of these unique methods can be found in Appendix D.

Previously Published As:

Some of the information contained in this book was previously published in the following Samarpan Alchemy Publications:

- *Chakra & Meridian Antidotes* (2009)
- *Vessel Antidotes* (2009)
- *Protection & Sanctuary Nets* (2009)

However:

- The information contained this book has been extensively re-written and extended, so that it is now more comprehensive than that found in those earlier books.
- These 3 earlier publications have now been withdrawn, and superseded by new Samarpan Alchemy Publications, of which this book is one example.

Real-Life Case Studies:

Many of the examples and case-studies contained in this book are drawn from real-life.

However:

- Wherever possible, permission for their inclusion has been obtained.
- Personal details have been changed to ensure that the privacy and anonymity of all the individuals is secured, without changing the meaning of the story itself.

C1. Introduction to Volume 1:

There is a well-known saying in therapy circles…

> *A therapist tends to attract clients with the same issues they themselves have had to deal with along their path of inner growth.*

For example, a good friend of mine had an issue with 'grounding'.

They had a long, hard struggle learning how to ground themselves, how to be comfortable in their own physical body, and they even found it hard to walk barefoot on green grass or along a sandy beach.

Fortunately, they found therapies and methods which helped them overcome this issue.

And now that they have conquered their fears around being grounded, they tend to attract those clients who also have similar issues around being grounded… and so their hard won experience, gained over a number of years, is being put to good use helping others struggling with the same personal issues.

When someone who has 'been there, done that, and got the T-shirt' gives you advice, it somehow carries greater weight than if it comes from someone who has got their advice, second-hand, from a self-help book, or even worse… a magazine article. That kind of advice, no matter how well intentioned, always comes over as a bit hollow.

Hard won experience counts… and this is what human beings do, we pass on what we have learnt… especially when it is the important stuff.

The same principle also applies to the teaching of spiritual and personal development.

To be effective, a teacher must first learn the developmental lessons they are going to teach and write about.

Here, I am not really referring to the teaching of academic subjects such as Maths, Physics or Geography... No, I am referring to all those lessons that challenge and change us... to all those areas which are often referred to as our *life-lessons.*[1] There is a wonderful observation by the American writer and teacher Alan Seale, where he states that if you can learn a life lesson in just under a week or a month then *it really wasn't a life lesson.* To learn a life lesson takes much, much longer... indeed, it may even take you a whole lifetime to learn and fully master.

With a life lesson, you usually need to 'fall over' several times before you start to see the unconscious patterns responsible... and so you need the involvement of many different people, across your lifetime, to help create the situations that 'teach' you about these unconscious patterns... and you also need inner patience, strength, humour and grace to struggle on with those unconscious habits and programming until you eventually change the patterns, learn the life lesson, and so end up 'transformed'.

When young, all of that sounds so depressing. Why do we have to devote so much time and energy in sorting ourselves out on t*he inside*... why can't we just devote our life to doing the things we want to do, and not be trapped by all the things that are holding us back? But the odd thing is, if you do start to engage with your life lessons, they often become intriguing... interesting... maybe even fascinating.

It's a bit like school homework, which you put off doing until the last minute, and then, once you eventually force yourself to sit down and do it, you suddenly find yourself drawn in and start to become

1 Although, for a few people, learning to cope with the issues around their schooling is indeed one of their life lessons. I know of one lady who has spent years getting over the way she was badly treated at school.

interested in the subject. If you were learning Maths, Physics or Geography there would be a variety of text books you could reference to help you along the way... and they would be properly titled and easy to find on the library bookshelves. However, when it comes to life lessons, it is often much harder to find the information that we need for our particular issue. And with a life lesson, it's often as much about *unlearning the old*, as it is about *learning the new*... and that can and will take time.

Now, the book that you are holding in your hand, that you have been gracious enough to open, is about *energy boundaries* and *personal energy protection*... Does this mean that these were a few of the author's life lessons, and that he learnt much of the information contained in this book the long and hard way?

You bet I did!

Much of the information contained in this book was learnt through difficult circumstances, over years and decades. In a sense, it contains some of the gold and silver which I have been able to mine from my life on this planet... and which I am now passing on to others in the hope that it will make *their life easier*.

Many of these lessons have been spread out across the first 50 years of my life, and have involved different individuals and situations... although as I look back now I can see the common threads that were woven through them all.

Of course, I could put my head in my hands and say, 'Why didn't I see that then, it was so obvious? If only I had known at age 21 years what I know now. I have wasted so much of my life when I could have been doing something better!'

But, from a completely different perspective, my life hasn't been 'wasted'... because I was gathering the experience I needed to learn my life lessons.

Indeed, if life is really all about learning, then the most important thing is that you learn the lesson before you transition off this planet. To me now, whether you learn your lesson in the first quarter of life, or the middle, or right at the end is really a secondary consideration. The most important thing is that you learn it and graduate successfully.

Someone who learns their life lesson when they are in their 30s is in a better position than someone who learns it in their 50s say... but both are much, much better than someone who passes over with the lesson unlearnt.

If you believe in reincarnation, then people who fail to learn their lesson have to come back to a new body and personality, and create new situations, where they hopefully can learn the lesson the next time around... or the next...or the next... In fact, these people will keep on coming back until the lesson gets learnt. That's what eternity is for.

So it took me until I was 50 to nail these issues... but my hope is that you may be able to do it much earlier in your cycle, using the information and processes contained in this book, and so reap the benefits earlier than I did.

In these *Energy Boundaries* books, Volume 1 & 2, you will find information relating to:

- The problems which can occur if you don't have effective energy boundaries.

- The problems which can occur as you struggle to create and maintain effective energy boundaries.

- The problems which can occur if your boundaries are too rigid and inflexible.

But it won't just be about theory... there will be plenty of practical stuff you can do to create and maintain effective energy boundaries... a whole range of different techniques, ideas and suggestions, designed for different personal situations.

Along with Volumes 1 & 2, there is also a free PDF, Volume 3, which you can download from my website... and at this stage, I cannot rule out the possibility of a Volume 4... because the subject of energy boundaries is just so **BIG**. And the problem of understanding the need for personal energy protection is not just because it is so big... it's also *multi-dimensional*... which is reflected in the structure and chapters of this book.

You see, it's not just about building an energy wall and then hiding behind it... Oh no, that would make it too easy. As we shall see, it's more about understanding the nature of the situation you are in and finding the right form of boundary for you in that moment.

In her book *Energetic Boundaries*, Cyndi Dale writes that:

> *At least two-thirds of the individuals I've seen in my intuitive-counselling practice have lacked energetic boundaries or had damaged boundaries. But by erecting and / or healing those boundaries, they have grown leaps and bounds.*[2]

Let's assume that, in her practice, Cyndi Dale is dealing with people with a whole range of different issues...

- People with issues relating to health.
- People with issues relating to money and abundance.
- People with issues relating to love and relationships.

---

2 Cyndi Dale, page 3.

These are what many counsellors and psychics refer to as the 'Big 3'... because the majority of people who go to see a psychic / counsellor are struggling with a variation upon one of those issues.

If this is the case, which it obviously is if you read the many examples in Cyndi Dale's book, then roughly 60% to 70% of our personal problems involve **some level of boundary issues**... and become easier to deal with if a person can establish strong and effective personal boundaries.

In this book, I will be making the distinction between a barrier and a boundary. A barrier is a wall which is solid and impenetrable, whereas a boundary is porous, and has the intelligence to allow through what is beneficial, and keep out what is harmful. In contrast, a barrier keeps everything out. A good example from popular culture is the Bond girl from the classic movie *Goldfinger* who was covered in gold paint, and died because her skin couldn't breathe. Although barriers will provide total protection, sometimes a boundary is better for us because it allows us to breath in some way.

When a boundary is working well, on whatever level (i.e. physical, emotional, mental or spiritual), then it will:

- Hold material and energy inside our personal space.

- Prevent external material or energy from penetrating / invading our personal space.

- Prevent material and energy from leaking out, or being taken / stolen.

- Allow into our personal space all material and energy which is beneficial for us, and keep out all material and energy which is harmful to us.

- Identify what is us from what is *not us.*

Sometimes boundaries are *physical*, like our skin, and sometimes they are more *virtual*, like our immune system, where anti-bodies are programmed to attack anything which is harmful, anything which is not perceived as being *us*. This kind of boundary is composed of the right information... and will fail if it is re-programmed with the wrong information.

Using these simple definitions, it is easy to see that when a boundary breaks down, chaos often ensues on that level, and quickly spreads. This is why Cyndi Dale is right when she says that the majority of personal issues have a boundary failure involved somewhere in the mix... and boundary failure on one level has a way of quickly spreading and infecting other levels of our being.

Because the subject is so big and multi-dimensional, it occurs in many different areas and contexts. If as Cyndi Dale believes 70% of issues contain a boundary element then:

- When someone has a problem with **money**, 70% of the time a boundary issue will be involved on some level.

- When someone has a problem with **love and relationships**, 70% of the time a boundary issue will be involved on some level.

- When someone has a problem with **health and wellbeing**, 70% of the time a boundary issue will be involved on some level.

And that is just the Big 3... there are lots of other types of issues as well which also include a boundary element. This is why Energy Boundaries Volume 1 & 2 look at the subject from lots of different angles and perspectives.

Now, many books on the subject of energy boundaries and personal protection approach the subject as if it is relatively straight forwards... and in a way *it is*... and in another way *it isn't*. The principles are relatively easy... but the contexts and situations can be vastly different, especially when human behaviour and beliefs can be so weird, diverse and contradictory.

For example, a few questions to consider:

- Does an energy boundary remain effective if the person who is being protected is also trying to tear it down from the inside (and why would anyone want to engage in such self-sabotage)?

- If someone is a preying on someone else's energy, does it make a difference if they are feeding on a total stranger, or someone within their own immediate family?

- How do your own personal issues and internal demons weaken your ability to defend yourself?

- How can modern electro-magnetic pollution weaken our ability to defend ourselves?

- How does our own energy relate to the energy in the environment around us, and how might this make us stronger or weaker?

- How can fake love and forgiveness undermine our ability to protect ourselves?

The answer to these questions might drastically change how you choose to protect yourself in a given situation. I have therefore attempted to write two books that not only provide you with a range of different techniques and methods to protect yourself... but through understanding the answers to the above questions, hopefully your ability to use these techniques and methods will also become more effective.

Because sometimes information is our best form of defence (and if you start to act upon that information that is when it turns into 'wisdom', and you start to really learn your current life lesson). This is why *Energy Boundaries* Volume 1 and Volume 2, explore the subject from a number of different angles and perspectives. Although it is not necessary to read Volume 1 & 2 in sequence, the information contained in Volume 2 does build upon Volume 1, because it contains subjects which take the reader deeper into the subject of energetic protection.

As you read this book, some of the chapters you will find interesting, some less so (although you may realise that although it doesn't apply to you, you do have a friend who is stuck in a similar kind of destructive pattern). However, some chapters may indeed push your mental and emotional buttons, when you suddenly realise *'That's me, I do that... that's the situation I am currently trapped in!'* And that's when you have a new opportunity to learn one of your life lessons, and stop being the victim.

This book has been written for the experienced energy therapist *and* the complete novice, who knows that they have a problem, but is new to the subject, and isn't sure where to start or what to do.

So there may not be books out here to help with *all* of life's lessons... but for those of us struggling with difficult boundary issues, I hope with this book the learning just got a little easier.

... And the fact you are reading this book is proof that the techniques contained within **do work**, because they are the ones I used to fix myself, and transform my life... and if that hadn't happened, I would never have been able to write, complete and publish this volume, and turn my life around.

Best Wishes!

Brian Parsons
Devon, March 2015

C2. Protection & Support, Active & Passive:

Within ICGT - the Institute of Crystal & Gem Therapy, the school in which I trained before becoming one of their tutors - the subject of energy boundaries is approached through an understanding of the difference between 'protection', and 'support'. Protection and support are two topics which are closely related, but are *not* identical.

Support:

Support is when, although you don't feel that you are under any external influence and there is no psychic attack taking place, you do feel the need for some external support, something to boost or enhance your own energy.

For example, when you need to go into your boss's office and ask for a pay raise. Unless your boss is Dracula, then you probably won't be requiring energy protection. However, you may require some vibrational support, something to boost your confidence, or perhaps enhance your communication skills.

Now, when it comes to advising what crystals, or other vibrational tools, are good for providing you with additional energy support, the answer is usually 'How long is a piece of string?' It is highly dependent upon the circumstances, and it is also highly dependent on the individual involved. Everyone is unique, and so there are no readymade, off the shelf solutions that will work for everyone.

Once again, going back to our example of asking your boss for a pay raise, what exactly is the issue which you need support with? Is it that:

- You lack *communication skills*, in which case you need crystals to enhance your eloquence... Turquoise, Blue Chrysocolla, or maybe Blue Lace Agate?

• You lack *self-worth*, in which case you need crystals to enhance your own feeling of being worthy of extra money... Rhodonite, Rose Quartz, Pink Tourmaline, or maybe Unakite?

• You are unable to stay *grounded*, in which case you need crystals that will help you to literally stand your ground while making your pitch for extra money... Black Tourmaline, Hematite, or maybe Smoky Quartz?

• You always feel *disempowered* when talking with your boss, in which case you need something that will enhance your own feeling of empowerment... Pyrite, Citrine, or Yellow Vesuvianite perhaps?

As you can see, the method of support will vary considerably, depending on the type of internal issue that you are dealing with. Because with support, we are not dealing with something influencing us from outside, we are dealing with something missing from *inside* of us, usually experienced as a feeling of *lack*... a lack of confidence, a lack of self-worth, or a feeling that you cannot speak clearly and with confidence about what is important to us.

The crystal, or other vibrational tool, helps you to fill in this missing vibration, so that you can effectively up your game and not be held back by your own internal issues. But this can only occur while you are wearing or using it, and so it cannot provide you with a permanent solution.[1]

Within each of the above categories, there are a range of different options available, and some of these will work better for some people, while others less so.

---

1 If you are looking for a permanent solution you will probably need to seriously engage with some kind of therapy or personal development programme, as many of these issues have their roots in our unconscious minds.

This is why it is important to muscle test, or dowse, in order to identify the option that is the best fit for you. More information on Dowsing and Muscle Testing can be found in the *Samarpan Alchemy Supplement Manul* (refer to Appendix D). However, if this is not possible, then I suggest you analyse your current issue using colour therapy. Each colour has different positive and negative qualities associated with it, so all you need to do to find the colour associated with your issue, is to have a colour chart and a good understanding of your issue. It is that simple.

For example, if you feel disempowered when speaking to your boss, if that is your issue, then the lack of empowerment is a negative yellow issue, and so wearing a yellow crystal, or even yellow clothes (and they don't even have to be visible, you could be wearing yellow underwear), will help to counter your feelings of lack in this area. More information on the positive and negative qualities associated with different colours is given in the *Samarpan Alchemy Supplement Manual* (refer to Appendix D).

Protection:

Now if 'support' is about boosting your energy, then 'protection' is all about protecting yourself from external psychic influence, coercion or attack.

When people talk about psychic attack, then they usually have an image in their mind of some kind of Dracula figure, ready to pierce their neck with his long fangs, and suck the life out of them. But this is very much a stereotype, and psychic vampires often dress and behave very, very differently. Indeed, they may be all sweetness and light on the surface, like Professor Umbridge from the *Harry Potter* books. I even once came across a psychic vamp who was an ex-pastor… all smiles, caring and considerate.

So it's not a case of how they look that gives them away, but how they make you *feel*.

If you meet up with them, and then minutes after they leave, you feel drained, tired, depleted, ungrounded or knocked sideways, than one possible solution is that you have been vamped. The more it happens, the more you can safely conclude that this is the answer. But remember, test out your theory. It's important not to jump to any conclusions as it needs to happen more than once to be proved valid, and it needs to be detrimental to the one who is 'giving' the energy.[2]

The reason why I say that it needs to happen 'more than once', and be detrimental, is that I have come across cases where someone has been in desperate need of energy, and their friend has given them a one-off boost to get them through the difficult situation. It never happens again, and so never develops into vamping. It's a bit like a one-off loan to tide you over until pay-day. And beneficial, ongoing energy transfer is part of the relationship between a mother and child throughout childhood. So there are times where an energy transfer is a healthy thing and, on some level, agreed to by all the parties involved. To say that energy transfer is always wrong is too black and white, and to try to prevent the flow of nurturing energy from mother to child would be a form of child abuse.

But if you feel drained each time you meet a specific person, and if you are totally wiped after each encounter... and they are not your child... well, that's another thing entirely.

In the majority of these cases, the person who is doing the vamping is not conscious of their 'feeding' activity, and may even take great offence if you were ever to point it out to them, strenuously denying that they are doing any such thing. It's just a habit which they will probably have acquired during childhood, and is something they are

2 Although it is debatable as to whether 'giving' is the right word to use in this context.

not consciously aware of doing.

You need to be careful about what you say to these types of people, because if you accuse them of anything, they will probably use what you say as another stick to beat you over the head with. Usually, there is a deep-seated neediness within them, which no amount of reason or words will fix or alter. It's usually better to fix yourself, so that they cannot feed off you, than to try and change them.

Instead of suffering from psychic influence / attack, it is usually more likely that your average person is suffering from electro-magnetic stress from all the electrical machine, devices and gadgets that now surround us all... and you would never accuse your fridge-freezer of being a psychic vampire. For these situations involving electromagnetic influence, support may not be enough, and some form of active protection may also be required. If there is also psychic influence taking place, I have found that electro-magnetic stress makes it harder for the other person to deal with the psychic stuff going on.

In addition to psychic feeding, people can also engage in 'psychic bullying'. This is where even though they are not directly draining the other person's energy, they make themselves feel better through energetically 'leaning' on the other person's aura, effectively 'pushing' them down. In effect, they are making themselves feel superior through making someone else feel inferior.

And there is also a type of energy bullying / psychic attack which can occur between Gay and Straight male and female individuals, which is made possible by the different energy / sexual polarity which exists between heterosexuals and homosexuals, regardless of physical gender. It is usually the homosexuals who come off worst when this happens, and you only need to look at societies and cultures down through the ages to find evidence of this kind of persecution. More information on these types of encounter, along with practical advice, is given in Nathaniel Reeves' book *Gay Polarity Tantra Volume 1*

(Samarpan Alchemy Publications).

After reading all of the above, which is actually not an exhaustive list, hopefully you have come to realise that psychic influence / attack can come in many different forms, and may require one of several different methods / strategies to counter. In fact, half the battle is often finding the most appropriate strategy to counter what you are dealing with.

It's a bit like martial arts and the various forms of self-defence. Each is founded upon a different philosophy, and so has a different and distinct approach. For example, the external martial arts rely on muscular strength, while the internal martial arts rely on an individual's own internal energy to defeat an opponent, and Japanese Aikido uses the opponent's own energy against them. Because of these differences, each specific martial art has its pros and cons, advantages and disadvantages. A martial artist, trained in several different disciplines, will use the skill most appropriate to the situation they find themselves in.

And we need to learn to do the same.

However, when it comes to psychic defence and energy boundaries, there are several general points that we can make at this stage:

1) Every human being is born with an internal defence system, designed to protect them from external psychic interference. If someone else has been able to circumvent this defence system, then the questions are *how* and *why*? You may need to erect some form of artificial energy boundary to protect you in the short-term, but this can only be a temporary solution. While the artificial boundary is in place, your priority should be fixing your own internal defences so that you don't need an artificial energy boundary.

There is a favourite saying of mine in this regards, 'What is the point of locking the door, if you are only going to leave the key under the mat. What is the point of leaving the key under the mat, if you are only going to tell everyone where you have hidden it?'

Your own internal defence mechanisms are only as strong and effective as you allow them to be. If you are sabotaging them in some way then they will be ineffective when you need them. The same as a locked door is ineffective if you give a potential burglar the key to open it. The only protection you would have left is the hope that the burglar is too polite to burgle you.

Mother Nature, God, the Tao, Great Spirit, the Universe has given us all the subtle armoury needed to defend ourselves from psychic influence / attack. But for various reasons – low self-esteem, negative childhood programming, desperate need to be loved etc. – we do not make the best use of our own defence systems, or we foolishly deactivate them for some misguided reason (i.e. 'But he / she wouldn't hurt me... because he / she loves me!')

Now, many of the strategies and techniques in this book will help you to create effective boundaries, and help evict some troublesome intruders. But none of these techniques and methods are as good as your own internal defence system, and so your objective must be to get that working again, so that you become less reliant on external aids, using them only when absolutely required.

To achieve this requires you to go on a quest to discover why your own internal defences are not working, which often leads to the discovery that you have sabotaged them in some way. If that is the case, then to get them working again usually requires that you to let-go of a cherished belief or limiting attitude to life.

2) Question – Which is the best at cracking a nut? A) a sledgehammer, B) a small hammer, or C) an atom bomb?

Well, the answer is that they *all* will work. However, A) is over-kill, will take more effort to use, and probably crush the nut in the process;

while C) is likely to kill everyone else in a 10 mile radius, so there won't be anyone left to eat the nut. Probably not what was originally planned.

It's not always a question of what will do the job, but also of what is the most appropriate for the situation at hand. So, once again, the moral of our story is that you need the right tools for the job, and the most powerful tool may not be the most effective at getting the job done right. Unfortunately, there is something about the human ego that likes the sound of going for the *most* powerful option, and if there is a 'big red button' involved we just can't wait to press it.

And to be honest, if you are being bullied, and feel completely powerless, then it's only natural to want to call in the biggest and baddest dude in the playground to protect you. That's one of the reasons kids join gangs.

But if you end up using a protection strategy that is not appropriate to your given circumstances, then like it or not, it will probably create unforeseen consequences down the line that you will need to deal with.

3) What types of protective wall are you trying to build?

There is an old Sufi tale about a king who was afraid of dying. So he built a palace with walls 10 feet thick, so that Death would never be able to enter. Then he realised that Death could always enter through the door or windows, so he had these blocked off as well, while he was safe inside. He was then entombed within his own mausoleum… and soon died of asphyxiation.

This is one of the reasons why our book differentiates between barriers and boundaries. A barrier won't let anything through, a boundary will because it is porous. Time and time again, nature chooses to create intelligent boundaries, and rarely creates an impenetrable barrier.

For example, the lining of our lungs is a boundary, it lets oxygen in and carbon-dioxide out. The lining of our intestines, large and small, are boundaries that allow nutrients to pass into our bodies, and waste protects to pass out. We could not exist in our physical forms without effective boundaries.

Many physical illnesses are caused when a physical boundary within the body starts to break down, or becomes confused. It no longer allows good stuff to enter, and holds on to the bad stuff, so that it cannot be removed. Diabetes is a classic example. It's not that there isn't enough sugar within the blood but that, without insulin, what oxygen there is cannot pass *through the cell wall*, from the blood, into the cell to power it.

But this isn't just true in nature and biology. I recently watched a TV programme, with the historian John Snow, who was exploring the southern edge of the Roman Empire, running through the Sahara deserts in Morocco and Tunisia. He found that, instead of building a massive wall, manned by thousands of soldiers to keep out the desert tribes, the Romans built small forts at regular intervals along their southern border. Instead of trying to create impenetrable barriers to keep nomadic tribesmen out, the Romans found it was much more effective to create a porous boundary that allowed them to control the flow of people across their borders, allowing them to charge taxes and import fees each time someone crossed over.

So the lesson from the natural world, and from history, is that it's better to create intelligent boundaries than it is to build impenetrable barriers; and although impenetrable barriers *may* indeed be the best option to begin with, it is wise to transform them into intelligent boundaries over time.

There are problems with creating impenetrable boundaries. One, they take a lot of effort to resource, for little or no reward. Two, they don't allow good stuff to enter. And three, as Sue Lilly always says, they smell of *fear*, because you only create a barrier if you are afraid of something on the other side, what you are desperately trying to keep out. So, although it may be wise to erect a barrier to protect you from a nasty something you are afraid of... and if you are working on a hospital quarantine ward, you would be foolish not to take such precautions... don't be fooled into thinking that your barrier will also transform your fears. The universe has a way of making us face our fears sooner or later... and so when your barrier is breached, or comes crashing down, you too will need to face your fears. If you have used your time wisely while behind the barrier, and learnt to deal with your fears, then you are well prepared. However, if you haven't been doing your homework, then when the barrier comes down, you are no better off than when you started.

Active & Passive Strategies:

The final thing that we need to mention in this chapter is the difference between **Active** and **Passive** support and protection strategies.

Within ICGT, an active strategy requires you to 'do' something for it to remain effective, while a passive strategy does not require any 'doing', but is usually a matter of you wearing something, or putting something in your pocket.

Active strategies can include physical actions, speech / mantras, or visualisations.

The main disadvantage of an active strategy is that you need to keep doing it in order for it to remain effective, while the main advantage of a passive strategy is that it will continue to work even when you are no longer conscious of it.

However, the main disadvantage of a passive strategy is that you will need to have acquired or purchased the objects you need, and you will also have to have them easily to hand when you need them...

which may not be the case, especially when you are travelling. In contrast, the main advantage of an active strategy is that, once learnt, it is always in your head, and so you can deploy it whenever and wherever you need it.

Therefore ICGT teaches that it is best to develop a range of different strategies, both active and passive, and so, across these two books, I plan to give you a range of different active and passive strategies to that you can become well-equipped and prepared for whatever life sends your way.

C3. Importance of Energy Protocols:

One of the most important things which any student of energy healing needs to learn on their training is how to set up a healing session safely for all involved... for themselves and their client(s). In fact, during the ICGT Certificate training course, this is considered to be one of the most important elements which a student needs to learn.

Beginner students often don't initially appreciate why this is so important, and just want to plunge head first into the actual healing, learning the different layouts and techniques. But those who do this are not doing themselves or their clients any favours, and tend to suffer from the effects of poor energy hygiene later on down the line. It really is important that, whenever you engage in any kind of energy healing, you follow the principles of good energy hygiene for your own sake and for the sake of your client.

Let's imagine that two middle-aged ladies, Glenda and Joyce, suddenly bump into each other in the centre of their town. They haven't seen each other for over 25 years. In fact, the last time they saw each other was on their last day of secondary school.

After having met by chance after so long, they decide to go for a coffee, have a chat and catch-up on old times. They have so much to discuss and share, because school seems such a long time ago, and so much has happened in their busy lives since then.

Over coffee and cake, Joyce happens to mention that she is taking anti-depressants, because of all the worry and anxiety she is currently suffering. Her husband has been unemployed for the last 2 years, and been unable to find suitable employment because many employers consider him to be too old, which has devastated his confidence. She is now the only breadwinner in their house, and all the stress and uncertainty has taken its toll upon their relationship. Fortunately,

Glenda is a qualified energy therapist and says that she can easily help Joyce during this difficult period, and she should book up for a session, which is what Joyce duly does. They arrange to meet up for a 1 hour healing session at Glenda's house a week on Tuesday, in the afternoon.

A week later, which turns out to be a glorious summer's day, Joyce turns up at Glenda's house for her first energy healing session. She is a little apprehensive, because she has never had any form of energy healing before, in fact, up until 2 years ago, she had rarely been to see her own Doctor. But Glenda's therapy room looks so cosy and beautiful, and Glenda is so good at putting her at her ease, that Joyce soon starts to relax, and lies down on Glenda's therapy couch to begin the healing session.

Now, at the start of this energy healing session, the diagram below shows us what is going on, on the conscious level, between Joyce and Glenda.

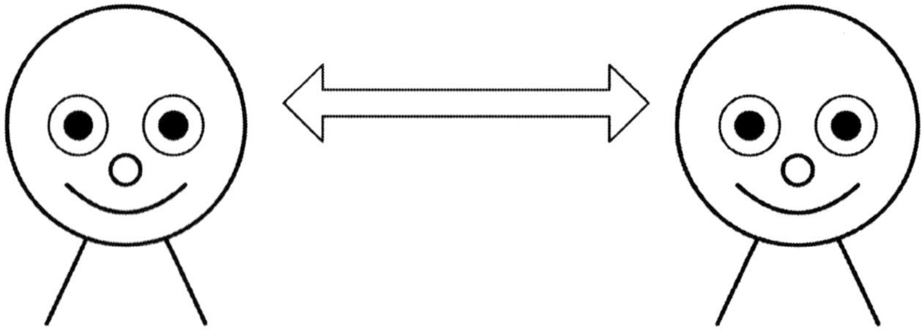

Figure 1: Joyce & Glenda – The Healing Session Conscious Level

As the energy healing session commences, on the surface everything looks calm and serene, and there appears to be nothing which might concern us... although we need to realise that as soon as Glenda starts to send healing energy to Joyce a 'door' opens between them, between their two energy fields, and when a door is open energy can flow both ways.

However, let us now lift the lid on the unconscious aspect of the interaction between them, and to fully understand that we need to go back in time 25 to 30 years, and replay various incidents which occurred to Glenda and Joyce while they were still at school together.

You see, back then, things weren't always smiles and happy sailing between them.

Glenda always resented Joyce for being the more beautiful of the two, and also for stealing all her boyfriends. In fact, Joyce's current husband originally started out as one of Glenda's boyfriends. Glenda always had a hard time attracting and keeping boyfriends, but for Joyce it came all too easily... In fact, Glenda is secretly happy that Joyce's marriage is currently 'on the rocks', and still harbours a lot of unresolved anger towards Joyce.

Joyce always resented Glenda for being the more intelligent of the two, and hated it when people asked, 'Why aren't you as clever as Glenda?' Joyce resents that Glenda was able to go to University, travel the world, and make a success of her life... while all Joyce got to do was marry a man who never amounted to much in his life, stay at home, and raise three children.

As we can now see, just underneath the surface, there is still a great deal of unresolved anger, bitterness and resentment between Joyce and Glenda.

But, from an energy healing perspective, why is any of this important? Well, when energy healing occurs between two people, between a therapist and their client, for it to work their two energy fields need to connect and merge to some extent. This is the equivalent of someone opening a door, and allowing the healer to enter into their energy field. If this didn't happen, if the two energy fields did not connect and overlap, then energy healing could not work.

But when a door is open, then you cannot always control what happens, or who enters... and when you open up your energy field to someone else, if you are not careful then you are also potentially opening yourself up to any negative energies contained within their aura. You may be expecting love and healing to enter, but instead you are gate-crashed by anger and resentment.

And vice versa, because they are also opening themselves up to any negative energies contained in your aura, energies which you may not even be aware of. Remember, a door opens in both directions.

So a better diagram to describe what is actually occurring between Joyce and Glenda, one which also includes the unconscious level, would look something like this:

Figure 2: Joyce & Glenda – The Healing Session Conscious & Unconscious Levels

In this diagram, we can see that when the 'energy door' is opened between Glenda and Joyce, all the anger and resentment, which they may not even remember or consciously acknowledge, can also start to flow between them... to the detriment of their own energy wellbeing.

In fact, this connection and overlap between two individual energy fields can occur in a number of similar professional encounters, not just during energy healing. It can potentially occur during other therapist / client relationships, including counsellors, masseurs, even hairdressers. Unfortunately, their training does not usually include the need for energy protection during or after a session, and so many of these professionals can go on to suffer burn out at some point in their career. Burnout occurs when an individual is trying to process, or resolve, psychic material which isn't theirs – i.e. like trying to resolve someone else's anger, or heal someone else's grief. It's impossible to do, because the emotion isn't yours in the first place.

This is why any reputable and grounded energy therapy always takes this unconscious interaction into account when setting up and undertaking any kind of healing or energy work on another human being... even when the therapist is not coming into direct contact with the client's physical body.

Also, remember the unconscious mind is believed to be 7 times larger and more powerful than the conscious mind, and so when we factor that fact into the energetic interaction between Joyce and Glenda, which is shown in this next diagram, we discover a potentially more toxic and unstable situation.

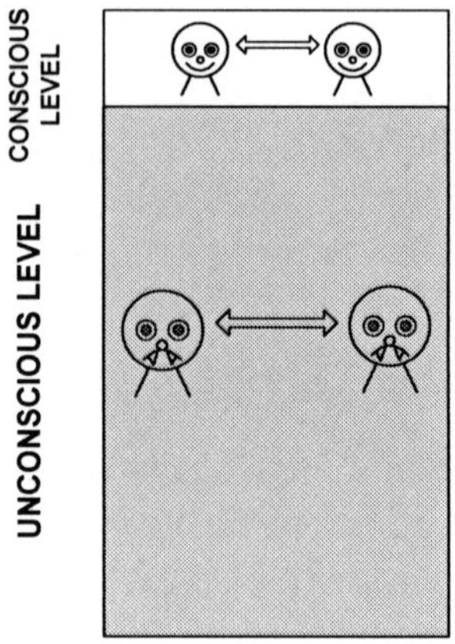

Figure 3: Joyce & Glenda – With correct proportions

As you can see, whatever is going on at the conscious level is nowhere near as 'big' as what might be going on at the unconscious level, which could have destructive consequences if tapped into… unless the therapist takes responsibility for the energy hygiene within the healing session, and prevents the unconscious mind(s) from creating havoc.

Now, none of this is meant to scare you, or prevent you from ever going to see an energy therapist (or counsellor, or hairdresser) ever again... or practising any energy therapy that you may have learned.

But I am trying to show you what needs to be factored in, what needs to be protected against, whenever an energy therapist and client connect and merge their two energy fields.

Basically, students learning energy healing need to be trained to:

- Ensure their energy is balanced and grounded before

commencing any healing session. The more balanced and grounded our own energy the less likely it is that we will project our own negativity on to our client, or that we will pick up / absorb our client's negativity into our own energy field.

• Put in place some kind of energy filter, which will prevent any negativity from passing between you. This is the same as putting some kind of security guard on the open door, to ensure that the wrong kind of people / energy does not enter. Also, because you are the therapist, it is important that you do this for yourself and for your client – i.e. you need to take safety responsibility for everyone who is involved in the session. Within ICGT, obviously we use crystals as our energy filters, selecting the one(s) which is most appropriate for that particular client and session. However, you could use other vibrational tools instead.

• Within ICGT, we always start a session by dowsing or muscle testing the question, 'Do I need any energy protection from my client, and does my client need any energy protection from me?' If the answer is yes to either or both of these questions then we dowse out an appropriate crystal to protect you the therapist, to wear during the session… and also a crystal to protect your client, which they will also wear during the session... and for anyone else who might also be in the room. Of course, you never say any of this out loud. Learning to dowse or muscle test silently is a good skill to acquire.

Any credible energy healing system will have developed similar methods to ensure that the therapist / practitioner is balanced and grounded at the start of the session, and that both parties are protected from any negative unconscious interactions. For example, if you are working on a child, and their parent is in the room with you, then you will need to include them in the energy interaction. You will need to ask 'Does the parent need any protection from the child… does the child need any protection from the parent?' It is not uncommon for parents to try and control their children, or for children to try to manipulate their parents, all at an unconscious level. Don't assume that you know what is going on... always ask the questions, always run through your pre-checks.

Note: Don't forget to retrieve any protection crystal off the client's body at the end of the session.

Now, if the answer to either of the protocol questions is a 'Yes' then don't panic. This doesn't make you a bad person. We all have unresolved negativity within us... it doesn't make us evil, it makes us human.

The trick is to own it, take responsibility for it, and not to try and dump it on to other people. I bet there are days when even the Dalai Lama wants to kick the cat... but he doesn't, and that's what makes him the Dalai Lama. He takes responsibility for his emotions and controls his negative impulses.

Another way of looking at it is as if someone were in a hospital ward with an infectious disease. The fact they have this disease doesn't make them evil, and so you shouldn't treat them as any less human. However, that doesn't mean that you shouldn't take sensible precautions, to ensure that you don't catch this disease, or prevent it from infecting anyone else. Also, you wouldn't want to give them any of your bugs, because in their weakened state their immune system might not be able to cope with even the common cold.

As we said at the start of this chapter, it's about learning the principles of good energy hygiene. It's a question of getting into *good energy habits...* which is why on an ICGT Certificate course we ensure students develop the right habits from the very beginning of their course.

Now, to be honest, this is something which I used to find a little annoying... (confession time coming up). You see, I was initially one of those people who saw the pre-checks as a 'hindrance'. I did them, but thought they were a waste of time, because the people I was working on didn't seem to be filled to the brim with negativity, and so I didn't understand why I needed to protect myself to such an extent.[1]

Then one day I got it, I finally understand why it was so necessary... and it came through reading a book on EMDR (Eye Movement Desensitization and Reprocessing) therapy, a therapy which has proven very effective in helping people suffering from PTSD (post traumatic stress disorder).

EMDR is a therapy which is very simple... and yet has a very complex set-up protocol, and the pre-checks are often more complicated and time-consuming then the therapy itself.

Initially, as I was reading this book, I couldn't get my head around why a therapy so simple would need a set-up protocol which was so complex...

That's when I finally got it... the light-bulb moment.

If you see 100 clients in a month, then 99 of those clients will be relatively normal, and your energy field will be able to handle their negativity with no problem. I am not saying this is a wise thing to do... but as a therapist you could get away with it for a while.

However, out of those 100, the last person to walk in the room might be suffering from PTSD, or is someone who was physically, sexually or emotionally abused as a child, or has been doing hard drugs for decades, or is psychotic...

When you plug into *their* energy field and they plug into *yours*, they'll wipe the floor with you.

---

1 The fact I am writting several books on the need for strong energy boundaries probably shows you how much I had still yet to learn in this particular area of life.

You will have developed no effective protection against such a high level of negativity, and so will have no defence against them...

...Unless you have set-up energy protection at the start of your session.

But to do that, you need to have got into the habit of doing so. And to do that, you can't treat this 1 person in the same way as the other 99 you saw earlier. You need to treat all of the 100 as if they were that 1 dangerous person who could wipe you out.

You need to use 'the habit' on everyone you see, every session you undertake, up until the moment you retire... and it is this good habit which keeps you safe.

This is why ICGT actively encourages people to get into the habit of energy protection at the start of our course... because good energy hygiene can keep you safe and protected.

In a hospital, the doctors and nurses are all required to wash their hands with antiseptic gel on a regular basis, and there are no exceptions. This creates good hygiene, and helps protect the patients (and staff) from any infectious diseases which may be doing the rounds. Any doctor or surgeon who believed themselves to be 'above all that', who were far too qualified to need to wash their hands, would be taken to one side by the hospital administrator, or ward nurse, and told a few home truths. Safety comes before ego.

Now if you get the chance to study a range of different energy healing systems, you will see that (hopefully) they all teach an energy set-up protocol which is designed to protect the therapist and the client. Although many of these protocols may be different, they will all share the same aim... protection and safety.

Because kinesiology uses muscle testing as its assessment method, which merges your energy field more deeply with your clients then say dowsing, kinesiology schools tend to have more complex set-up protocols then crystal therapy schools, which utilise dowsing as their primary assessment method.

Another reason why being grounded and balanced is so important is that, unless you are, the client's unconscious mind may be capable of throwing off your particular assessment method... especially if you are taking them to a place where they just do not want to go. For example, if you are working on a client who has issues to do with self-love, and the client's unconscious does not want to explore those issues, then if you are ungrounded their unconscious mind might be strong enough to influence your pendulum into giving you the wrong answers, which means the healing session will be ineffective. Don't ever assume that someone else cannot influence your pendulum if you are unprotected and / or ungrounded. It has been shown that if you are ungrounded, then they can.

Now, if you have been reading this section thinking, I am not an energy therapist, this is not something I will be using... think again.

Set-up protocols help to ground, balance and stabilise your own energy, and so can be used whenever you need to deal with someone whose energy is dodgy, or where you need some extra protection, or a boost of confidence.

Basic protocols to help anyone keep their energy balanced and grounded are given in the *Samarpan Alchemy Supplementary Manual* (refer to Appendix D).

But once again, they will only work if you *remember to do them*, and so it's all about acquiring *good habits*.

Final Word:

Also, we need to quickly mention the 'close down' protocol.

Within ICGT, we also teach that it is good idea to have a little close down protocol as well.

Most credible therapies have a protocol or ritual which they use to bring a session to an end.

This is to ensure that your two energy fields separate out, and you close the door on one another. It's a way of ensuring that your body and theirs *knows* that the healing session is now at an end, and you have come back to a space where you are both 'separate' individuals.

Otherwise, you may still be 'connected' 24 hours after the session ended, which is not a good thing to be.

This 'close down' ritual doesn't need to be too elaborate, and I often encourage students to devise their own.

Usually, it is a simple as spraying an essence on the palms of each hand, gently passing your hands through their aura, and silently repeating a phrase 'This session is at an end... we separate with love.'

Once it is lodged in your unconscious mind, you don't even need to use the essence... performing the hand movements is enough to initiate the seperation of your two auras.

But, once again, it is a good idea if you get into doing that at the end of your healing sessions. It's another good energy hygiene habit to get into.

C4. Personal Demons:

One of the ways in which other people crawl inside our heads, discover how we tick, and so discover interesting and clever ways to manipulate us is through our personal issues... which I prefer to call our *personal demons*.

This is the basic ABC of brain-washing... and most therapies to be honest. Because you need to discover how someone's head works, what they think and believe, and most importantly what they desire and need, before you can start to change and shift their behaviour.

However, the difference between brain-washing and therapy is that the therapist is meant to have your best interests at heart, and is trying to change you into a happier, more emotionally well-adjusted individual. The brain-washer doesn't care one jot about you as an individual, and whether you are happy or not, but just wants to manipulate you to obediently follow their script, and behave in the way they want you too.

For all those of you who think that no one can ever be brain-washed into behaving against their own true nature, then all I need to do is point you in the direction of:

- The *Stockholm Syndrome*, also known as 'capture-bonding', where hostages start to express empathy and sympathy towards their captors, even developing positive feelings towards them, and in extreme cases even willingly follow their orders.

- The 1960s film *The Manchurian Candidate* was based on the true stories of U.S. servicemen, returning from the Korean war, who had been brainwashed into accepting the total supremacy of communism as a political system. At the time, the thought that the Chinese could take your average American male citizen and turn his mind against his own country was something which U.S. politicians found truly terrifying. To find out how the Chinese did it read Robert B. Cialdini's book *The Psychology of Influence and Persuasion*. Hint: No torture was involved, just a good grasp of human psychology.

For example, if someone was seriously trying to brainwash you, trying to work out how you think at a conscious and unconscious level in order to break down your defences so they can re-build you to suit their purpose, one of the first things they would do is work out if you were an *introvert* or *extrovert*.

An introvert finds meaning within their own head, and so needs to spend some time each day, alone, so that they can mentally re-charge. To break down an introvert, you never leave them alone, you never give them the quiet time they need to re-enter their inner world, and you constantly surround them with other people. As John-Paul Sartre once said 'Hell is other people'. That's how you break an introvert.

An extrovert finds meaning through their social interactions with other people and so they need to spend time talking and conversing with others. To break down an extrovert, you do leave them alone with their own thoughts, and you keep to an absolute minimum their ability to connect with other people (i.e. you push the food into their cell through a small hatch, so all they ever get to see is a human hand). That's how you break an extrovert.

Now what I have just outlined may sound like something out of George Orwell's famous novel *1984*, something that is confined to cults, terrorist organisations, prisons, the army, or the Secret Service. However, think again. It actually can occur much closer to home (although not in such an extreme form).

If you think back to your early childhood, and the different strategies your parents used to raise you then 'Go to your room and think about what you have done', or 'You need a time out on the naughty step', or 'Stop sulking in your room and go outside and play with Tom' can be seen as ways to control an infant introvert or extrovert.

But you also find it in office politics:

"John, I know you like working on your own, but for the next six months, you're going to have to join this big team because we have an important project to complete..."

"Paul, I know you're really a team player, but for the next six months I need you to work on your own, because it's the only way we're ever going to complete this project on time..."

When this happens, it may be completely innocent, and vital to the success of the project / organisation. But I have also seen it happen enough times to know that, although the manager isn't trying to break the employee's spirit, often they are trying to show the employee who is the real 'boss' and work allocation is one of their most effective weapons to achieve this.

If this were to happen to you, then your best defence is to remain conscious of what is going on, and find other ways to *feed your need.* It's really the classic 'You can't change the situation, but you can change how you respond to the situation'.

Remember, you don't spend all your time at work (even though it may seem like you do), and so during your free time, you can give yourself exactly what you are being denied at work. For example, the introvert can go home and read a good book, and the extrovert can arrange to join a new and exciting line-dancing or salsa group. If you just stand back, and take a fresh look, there are usually ways which you can keep yourself sane.

OK, if you are a small kid then your options are severely limited. But when you grow up and become an adult then you do have the option to change your behaviour and response patterns. So don't ever think that you are a victim of your upbringing.

But the next way in which people try to control you is through your personal demons. Basically, they try and use your own emotions against you.

For example:

- If you are someone who is prone to **anger**, then they create situations that make you angry. Then they can either be the person who you are angry towards, or the person who sympathises, and tells you that your anger is justified and how you have been treated badly. Although anger, used rightly, is a self-defence mechanism, it can also make you predictable and easy to manipulate.

- If you are someone who is prone to **fear**, then they create situations that make you feel afraid. If you feel fear then you will want to avoid your fears, and run away and hide. If they are the person who helps you cope with your fears, then you may become totally dependent on them, which they can then use to their advantage (i.e. If you don't do this for me, then I'll walk, and then where will you be?)

- If you are someone who is prone to **guilt** and **low self-worth**, then they create situations that make you feel guilty. If you feel guilty, then you usually spend all your time trying to make things right and perfect, or apologising for being so useless when you fail to achieve perfection. Either way, they are the ones in control of the situation, and you are continually playing catch-up.

- If you are prone to **worry and anxiety**, then they will create situations that make you worry, make you anxious. If you are worrying about a situation then you will be totally preoccupied with thinking about it, 24/7. When this happens, you don't have time to consider what else is going on in your life, which is what they want, because they can get up to mischief behind your back. It's classic misdirection.

• If you are someone who is prone to **loneliness**, then they will create situations where you are afraid of being alone. According to Attachment theory, we all have a deep-seated, primal need for an emotional connection to at least one other human being, and when that connection is either under threat, or has become severed completely, we can behave in stupid and irrational ways, trying to re-establish an emotional connection once again. So if we are crippled by loneliness, or the fear of loneliness, and someone comes into our life, offering us the potential for a relationship / emotional connection, then how far will we go, what will we do, in order to keep them in our life? This can also occur if your personal demon is one of **grief** or feeling **unloved**, where you will do almost anything in order to feel loved by someone else.

• If you are someone who is prone to feelings of **rejection**, then they will create situations where you are afraid of being rejected. This is similar to the need for emotional connection. If someone comes into our lives, and offers us the possibility of acceptance, after a lifetime of constant emotional rejection, then we'll probably jump at the chance of a relationship with them. But then that gives them real power over us, because each time we don't toe the line, they can threaten to withdraw their acceptance, plunging us back into a new cycle of painful rejection, which we will try to avoid at any cost. This can also occur if your personal demon is **approval**, where you need the approval of someone else to validate you in some way.

• If you are someone who is prone to **jealousy** or **envy**, then they will create situations where we are jealous or envious of others and what they have. Jealousy is where you have lost something and you desperately want it back. Envy is where you lack something you see that other people have, and you desperately want it as well. Either way, someone can manipulate your feelings of jealousy / envy, allowing you to believe that if you do exactly what they want you will obtain your desire. This can also occur if your personal demon is one of **desperate need**, where you don't just want something but you need it, desperately.

- If you are someone who is prone to **shame**, feelings that you are a bad person, then they will create situations where you feel bad about yourself. Shame is the real killer of self-worth. It's not that you've done something bad, but that you are 100% a 'bad person'. Shame totally annihilates any positive self-image you may have. So if we are afflicted by shame, and someone comes into our life who makes us feel good about ourselves, who helps us to validate our existence, then just a bad word from them, or even a disapproving look, can often send us plunging back into the black hole of shame.

Do you see how it works?

Newspapers frequently run stories about women who have been conned out of their life's savings by a sweet-talking conman, who totally convinced them that they were in love, and about to get married... Only before he can marry her, he needs to clear a £50,000 business debt which is hanging over his head. And she is so desperate for the marriage to happen, and their dream life to start, that she lends him the money... and then he vanishes never to be heard of again.

Now as you read this you are probably thinking 'What an idiot she was, I would never fall for a scam like that...', and you probably wouldn't, because you don't feel lonely, you don't have a desperate need to be loved. But don't be fooled that this doesn't mean that you can't be conned. We all have something in our unconscious which can be manipulated or exploited. If a conman was going to con you, then they would spend time sizing you up, discovering what your particular personal demons were, your weaknesses, and then devise a completely different strategy to get you to give them the £50,000.

For as one top conman says in Kevin Dutton's book *Flipnosis: The Art of Split Second Persuasion*:

> *I'll find out everything [I can about the person]. From how they do business to what they do on the weekend. Top athletes study videos of their opponents, dissect their game. I do the same: gather information, start building up a picture of who I'm dealing with. It's not rocket science. The more you know about someone, the more the odds are stacked in your favour... I'm like a surveyor. But instead of buildings I do minds.*[1]

In one sense, even though the basic emotional motivations are all too familiar, each con is a *custom job*.

But don't worry. First they would discover if you had sufficient money in the bank to make their investment of time in your deception worthwhile. So if you don't have £50,000 in the bank, you're probably safe from a financial conman.

However, that doesn't mean that you are safe from other types of conmen who want something completely different from you. Not all conmen are only after your money.

In my own life, and not taking up too much time with the boring details, I once had something taken away from me while working for a particular company.

I can see now that, as the Mafia say, *it wasn't personal, just business*. It was just a lot of senior managers playing politics, engaging in inter-departmental warfare, and I was just collateral damage, which they didn't care about for one moment.

1 Kevin Dutton, p. 292 to 293.

But I felt this loss very deeply because it struck at the core of who I believed I was, and as a consequence I wanted it back… badly… very badly… very, very badly… and so for a period, I was prone to jealousy and envy.

As a consequence, this made it very easy for those senior managers to manipulate me, because all they had to do was dangle a juicy carrot in front of my eyes, suggesting 'There may be a way to get back what you have lost', and when they did that, they had my total and undivided attention. If they went on to say 'If you were to do X, then it may be possible to get back Y', then guess who went completely overboard to complete X?

But as Nietzsche says, 'Whatever doesn't kill you makes you stronger'… and so eventually I came out the other side of this whole experience a wiser and stronger individual (and the book you are reading now would not have come about if it weren't for that whole experience).And, as a consequence of that awful experience, many of the techniques in this book were tested while under active enemy fire.

How did I manage it? Well, as we have said, once someone has identified your personal demons, of which you may be largely unconscious, then they effectively have power over you. It becomes much, much easier for them to manipulate and influence you to do what they want. And you don't want that now, do you?

In the ancient magical traditions, if someone knew your true and secret 'name' then they had power over you, which is why that name had to be kept secret, shared only with your most trusted friends and family (… and maybe not even then).

The principle here is very much the same. But instead of 'secret name', instead insert the words of your emotional and personal 'demons'. If someone can work those out, then they also have power over you.

Basically, they will have identified which of your emotional buttons they need to press to get you to behave in the way they want.

So what you need to do to prevent this, to remove any power they have over you, is to either de-activate that emotional button, so that it will no longer work... or hide it, so that they can no longer find it and press it.

To help you defuse or hide your emotional buttons, below is a list of *Crystal Antidotes* which can help you do just that. A *Crystal Antidote* is two or three specific crystals, which when brought together, create a vibration which helps to transform a negative energy, limiting emotion or issue. They transform the negative energies associated with these issues into positive energies, so removing the emotional buttons.[2] See the *Samarpan Alchemy Supplement Book* for more information on Crystal Antidotes and the different was they can be applied.

OK, this may only be temporary, or maybe something which you use continually to keep yourself safe, but it is a lot better than being open and emotionally vulnerable. This list isn't exhaustive, and there are many of other emotional issues which can also leave you susceptible and open to external influence, but these are probably the most common culprits.

Antidote Issue	Required Crystals
Anger	Red Carnelian Moonstone Blue Sapphire
Desperate Need	Heliodor Red Jasper Lapis Lazulli

2 The Fear Antidote comes from Dorothy Roeder's book *Crystal Co-Creators* (Light Technology Publishing, 1994). All the other Antidotes were developed by myself.

Antidote Issue	Required Crystals
Envy	Amazonite Yellow Chrysoberyl Pietersite
Fear	Amethyst Kunzite Tanzanite
Grief	Red Coral Rose Quartz Sodalite
Guilt	Charoite Malachite Orange Citrine
Jealousy	Rhodonite Sodalite Sunstone
Loneliness	Yellow Fluorite Red Garnet Sodalite
Rejection	Moss Agate Dark Blue Apatite Pyrite
Shame	Yellow Apatite Lapis Lazulli Clear Quartz
Unloved	Pietersite Sugilite Sunstone
Worry & Anxiety	Amethyst Orange Citrine Turquoise

Table 1: Crystal Antidotes for Specific Issues

C5. Your Heart Protector Meridian:

Fortunately, our individual subtle energy body is not without its internal defence systems, which can protect us and keep us safe from psychic influence and manipulation... *but only if they are functioning correctly.*

Within the meridian system, the most important of these is the Heart Protector meridian (also known as the Heart Constrictor meridian, or the Circulation-Sex meridian). Personally, I prefer to use the name Heart Protector meridian because it points to its primary role and function, to protect the Heart from psychic influence and intrusion from external parties.

In Chinese philosophy and medicine, our Heart is believed to be the most important organ of the body. It is considered to be the seat of our Soul and Mind, our energetic core and centre, all of which are *not* considered to lie within the realm of our Brain. We now know that it is the Heart, and not the Brain, which generates the largest electromagnetic field of any organ within the body, so if there is any organ responsible for generating and maintaining our aura then it would most likely be the Heart. The Heart is the most powerful and pumped up organ of the body.[1]

The Ancient Egyptians also believed the Heart was the most important organ within the body, which is why they went to such pains to preserve it during the mummification process. The Brain they just threw away.

It is interesting how many ancient civilisations regarded the Heart to be more important than the Brain. Today, now that we are aware of what the Brain does, modern science just assumes that these ancient civilisations were blind and ignorant of the facts... but what if it is we

1 Which means the intelligent machines in *The Matrix* movie trilogy got it so wrong when they used human brains as their primary power source.

who are missing something quite important, something that to our ancestors was blindingly obvious?

To understand the difference between the Heart and the Brain, it is perhaps useful to use the phenomenon of electro-magnetism as an analogy. The Brain generates thought, which is like electricity, and the Heart generates a magnetic field, which is equivalent to our emotional states. Modern science teaches us that electricity and magnetism are two sides of the same phenomenon, which is known as an electro-magnetic field, and that electricity can create magnetic fields, and magnetic fields can create electricity. It's a two-way process, and it is the basis for much of our modern technology.

Now, science has also shown that our Brain / thoughts can influence our Heart / emotions and our energy field. Is it therefore too big a step to consider that the Heart's magnetic field might not also be able to influence and control the type of thoughts that the Brain generates?

And if a culture was more orientated towards the spiritual, such as the Ancient Egyptians and Chinese, then it would not be a total surprise to discover that they would place less emphasis upon the Brain's ability to think, and more upon the Heart's ability to love and magnetically influence the Brain?

But, if true, this means that whoever can control the Heart's energy fields, can also influence what thoughts / beliefs manifest in the Brain. This is why the Heart needs to be protected from external influence… because it is effectively the 'back-door' into our Mind. The Heart literally stores the vibrational patterns which our thoughts and beliefs are based upon.

The ancient Chinese likened all the 12 meridians to officials within the imperial court, giving them different roles and status. But for them, the Heart could only be linked to one individual… the *Emperor*, the most powerful and important person in the whole of the land.

But where does an Emperor live?

Does he live in a mud-brick hut, without guards, on the edge of the empire, from where he might be kidnapped by any passing nomadic tribe, who would then have direct influence and control over the empire?[2] No. The Emperor lives in a fortified palace, surrounded by guards, generals and armies who have all sworn to defend him... and the same is also true for our Inner Emperor, the Heart organ and Heart meridian (which together makes up our Heart space).

Within the meridian system, three meridians are given the specific task of protecting our Heart from external influence. These meridians are:

The **Triple Warmer meridian** (also known as the Triple Heater meridian, or the Triple Burner meridian), is responsible for our survival mechanism, our primary defence systems, and our fight / flight / freeze response. It scans our external environment for potential danger, whether real or imagined.

The **Small Intestine meridian** controls our ability to differentiate between reality and illusion, truth and lies, sincerity and falsehood. Without the protection of the Small Intestine meridian, it would be impossible to know when someone was trying to deceive us. It is our truth filter and gauge. However, unfortunately, the Small Intestine meridian does not become fully operational until around the age of 2 years, at which point a child starts to understand the concept of lying and deception. Before this occurs, the child is totally defenceless and accepts everything it is told as being 'truth', which is why adults can do so much damage, filling their child's head, when still a toddler, with their own 'version' of the truth. Once the Small Intestine meridian does become operational, it can only measure the truth against the ideas / beliefs that the child was given at an earlier age, so crooked

2 History is littered with tales of royal folk who were captured, and then ransomed back to their families for an extortionate amount of gold and silver.

parental beliefs are passed on to the next generation, which is how indoctrination within families occurs (and within societies, cultures, countries, religions, etc, etc). For example, if a baby is indoctrinated with the belief that 'all women are inferior' then, as a child and later an adult, it will tend to reject any evidence to the contrary, because this belief in 'female inferiority' has already been planted deep within its Heart space. Once a thought has gained access to our Heart space it becomes much harder to change or evict it.

In his book *Flipnosis: The Art of Split Second Persuasion*, Kevin Dutton quotes some interesting research studies that reveal the primary setting for our brain is to believe first, and to disbelieve second. Basically, human beings are born ready to believe anything they are told, and they have to learn to disbelieve. This means that if you want someone to believe whatever it is you are selling, all you need to do is shut down their unbelief anti-bodies, and their natural tendency will be to buy into your view of the world.

And the third meridian assigned to protect our Heart from external influence is ... yes, you've guessed it... the **Heart Protector meridian**.

Which means that, energetically, the three meridians you would need to knock out, in order to shut down Dutton's unbelief antibodies would by the Heart Protector, Small Intestine, and Triple Warmer meridians (although maybe not in that order).

We have already discussed how the Heart generates the most powerful of all the electro-magnetic fields within the physical body, which means that, energetically, it is the juiciest part of our subtle body, and so you wouldn't want just anyone strolling into your energy field and taking a 'snack' whenever they chose.

But then, neither do we want the Heart to be completely closed and walled off, because then we would be unable to share our warmth, our love, and the uniqueness of who we are with someone else. Because, according to *Attachment theory*, (which is probably one of the most successful attempts to explain why human beings do what they do when in relationships), our need for an emotional connection with another human being is one of the most important drives that we humans possess.

So we are at risk if we are too open, and in emotional pain if we are too closed.

In the real world, we therefore need some kind of protection that we can raise and lower, appropriate to the situation we find ourselves in. This is where the Heart Protector meridian comes in.

I always describe the Heart Protector meridian as being like a 'drawbridge' on a medieval castle, which we can raise and lower, as needs must. The innermost part of the castle represents the innermost part of our Heart, the juicy, warm, sacred bit. We can raise the drawbridge (Heart Protector) whenever we sense that an enemy is close-at- hand, thus closing down access to our inner self. We can also lower it when we feel that we are in the presence of people whom we love and trust, so that we can share our love, warmth and uniqueness with them (and vice versa).

However, the problem arises with the Heart Protector when the metaphorical hinges on which the drawbridge move, or the ropes that raise / lower it, become damaged in some way, and the mechanism no longer works correctly. Either the drawbridge remains open and cannot close, or it remains permanently closed, and cannot be opened.

Unfortunately, when this happens, we remain open to those who would harm us, and who come to see us as an easy meal, or closed to people who we want to love and trust but cannot emotionally connect with (and who then, unfortunately, start to believe that we are emotionally cold, unresponsive, closed off, or just not interested).

Why should this be?

Well, in Chinese medicine, the Heart Protector meridian is associated with our psychic 'radar', our psychic 'early warning' system. The Heart Protector is meant to help us differentiate between friend and foe, and help us to know who we should let in to our Heart space, and who we should slam the door on. Unfortunately, if the radar associated with the Heart Protector is a little off, then the whole process is thrown into disarray, and we cannot tell friend from foe, we do not know who to be open or closed too. But do not despair. It is possible to re-train the Heart Protector meridian, and we will explore how very soon.

However, my own research has led me to conclude that our 'psychic radar' is the Triple Warmer meridian *and* the Heart Protector meridian working in conjunction. Because of this, it is only when the Triple Warmer is prepared to power down, that the Heart Protector can also lower its defenses. While the Triple Warmer still senses potential danger in the external environment, the Heart Protector cannot lower.

There are also certain professions where the Heart Protector meridian, over time, can become locked into a certain 'state', either too open or too closed.

To be an effective counsellor or therapist requires that the Heart Protector remains open while seeing a client, because it helps the therapist to empathise with the client, helps them to understand the client's emotional drives and needs, helps the therapist to see the world from the client's point of view. However, counsellors / therapists can spend so much time with their Heart Protector open, that they lose the ability to close it down at the end of the working day, and so they remain completely open when they should be closed (i.e. at the supermarket checkout, picking the car up from the garage, walking down the main street of town). If they are wandering around town with their Heart open and exposed, is it any wonder that this can lead to emotional burnout? Also their inability to disconnect often means that their family / friends complain that they 'bring their work home with them'. They should be emotionally present for their family and friends, but instead they are emotionally distant or drained.

However, at the opposite extreme are surgeons, police, firemen, some doctors, and the Armed Forces, who need to be able to disconnect from their feelings, and other people's emotional baggage, if they are to perform their jobs successfully. This is especially important if they are required to interact with dangerous, violent, disturbed, and / or unpredictable individuals, whose energy you wouldn't want sloshing around inside your Heart space. When dealing with these types of people, it is best if your Heart Protector is firmly closed. But then, the issue is, when the policemen or fireman goes home to their partner and family at the end of their shift, can they open up again, can they let their family and friends back into their Heart space. Or do they remain closed, which means they come across as cold, rigid, and unfeeling.

When the hinges on the Heart Protector drawbridge are well oiled, and working smoothly, then the Heart Protector will open / close when we need it to, and we are well served and protected. But when the hinges are rusted, and the Heart Protector becomes locked in a single position, then we are at a major personal and social disadvantage.

Recently, there have been several books published on the subject of psychopaths, and the *positive* advantages of being one. It is believed that, because a psychopath can cut through the emotional limits that often leaves the rest of us floundering, they can be more effective in certain situations. Personally, my gut feeling is that the Heart Protector meridian has an important function within the whole good versus bad psychopath question, and whether there are degrees of the psychopathic. However, that is a discussion for another time and book.

The Heart Protector is also linked to the one of our most powerful human drives and motivations – sexuality and procreation.

Remember, one of its other names is the Circulation-Sex meridian, and it is associated with our ability to see ourselves as desirable, and to communicate our desirability to those who we may also desire.

But there is a problem with this, especially for women. Within ICGT it has been observed that when a woman has sex with a man, it is usually no big deal, she is able to maintain her energy boundaries around him, and maintain a sense of her own individuality (unless there are other emotional issues going on in her head). However, after she has given birth to her first baby with that man, that is when her defences all seem to lower automatically, the man is able to get inside her Head / Heart in a much deeper way, and she has a much harder time keeping him out and at bay.

Now, why would this be the case? Well, I think we can blame evolution and the selfish gene for this one.

The theory of the selfish gene states that our physical bodies are merely vehicles that allow genes to pass from one generation to the next. Forget literature, forget art, music, religion, and Sumo wrestling, our genes don't care anything about the many achievements of human civilisation. They're just concerned at hopping from the next penis into the next womb, ad infinitum (with the occasional variation in vehicle design along the way).

So evolution and our genes have a vested interest in getting a male and female to engage in sexual activity, otherwise there will be no next generation, and the genes will hit an evolutionary dead end.

Now, one of the things that advertisers the world over know is that 'sex sells', although, what advertisers use to sell their products in Saudi Arabia or Iran, I have no idea.

As Kevin Dutton also observes in his book *Flipnosis: The Art of Split Second Persuasion*, not only does 'sex sell', advertisers now know that just using the word 'sex' on the front covers of magazines and newspapers will grab someone's eye, and so boost circulation.

Advertisers have discovered this magic formula, that they use time and time again, because if they can stimulate a sexual response within the viewer, even if that response is unconscious and relatively mild, then this will result in the Heart Protector meridian lowering its defences, allowing the advertiser's message to reach the Heart space of that individual.

In the modern world, because advertisers overuse subtle sexual messages in adverts, leading to a constant bombardment of sexual messaging, this means that the vast majority of Heart Protectors are under continual stress and strain.

But why does the Heart Protector meridian automatically lower when we engage in, or think about, sex?

Well, the advertisers are taking advantage of a 'trap-door' built into our unconscious mind to ensure that procreation takes place, and the next generation is procreated.

If a man meets a woman, and they don't connect on a personality level, then their Heart Protectors remain firmly shut, and the chance of their giving birth to the next generation is slim to non-existent (and their genes will end up in their graves without ever had the chance to make copies of themselves).

But if a slim spark of sexual desire is ignited in either or both of them, then their Heart Protectors automatically lower, and the chance of them conceiving a baby becomes that much greater. Of course, when they wake up the next morning, having come to their senses, they probably believe that they made a terrible mistake. But by then it is too late, the sperm are already frantically swimming towards the egg, and one of those sperms has a date with destiny. This, then, is the energy mechanism behind the famous declaration 'Man, you won't believe what happened to me last night!'

But, once a woman has had one baby with a man, it is in the interest of evolution and the selfish genes to keep her Heart Protector permanently lowered in relation to her 'mate', because then the chances are greater that he will be able to father even more children with her. Literally, he has been given the keys to unlock her 'drawbridge'. However, this puts the woman at a distinct disadvantage, because if her Heart Protector is continually lowered in relation to this one man, then not only can he get inside her Head / Heart more easily, but she will be unconsciously be looking for a deeper emotional connection and response from him... one which he may be incapable or unwilling to provide... and that is when the incompatibility fireworks start.

So if a woman is trying to reclaim her power from a man, rebuilding her energy boundaries, and if the man is also the father of her children, then a healing and rebalancing of the Heart Protector, on some level, will need to take place. I think this is one of the reasons why the average woman has a harder time getting over a divorce then the man.

It is probably relevant that the ancient meaning behind the astrological sign of Virgo wasn't the young virgin, but that of a prostitute. However, this was a prostitute who, having had sex with a man never, ever gave her power away to him. In her head and heart, she always remained pure and virgin.

Another situation where the Heart Protector probably requires major healing is when someone has been sexually abused at an early age. From what I have seen, the Heart Protector meridian doesn't fully come on line until the start of puberty, after which the teenager should be able to explore intimate relationships, and their sexuality, from a place of confidence and security. Their ability to desire and be desirable is flowing well, and their psychic radar is switched on, knowing who to approach, and who to steer clear off.

There is strong psychiatric research from the United States that not all children go on to suffer from sexual abuse. Some children seem to take it to heart, and suffer deep sexual and emotional pain from the abuse, while others seem to be able to somehow brush it off, and go on to live apparently unaffected lives. However, these findings are very, very controversial, and go against all that the mass media and our politicians would like to believe, especially around the fragility of children. Because of this, the researchers who published these findings, and the American Psychological Association who supported them, came in for severe criticism by U.S. politicians. However, these findings have now been corroborated by a different research team.

However, if sexual abuse occurs *before* the Heart Protector meridian is allowed to fully form then it effectively gets trashed, remains either permanently open or closed. This creates either ineffective or inappropriate personal boundaries, and the individual is unsure who to let in or who to keep out, which can cause them massive personal and social problems in adulthood.

Once again, if such adults are to ever establish heartfelt, stable and loving relationships, then their Heart Protector meridian will need to be balanced and healed at some point.

Finally, there is another group of people who require our attention and consideration. Those who have become exposed and / or addicted to online pornography, which now, thanks to the internet, is happening at an earlier and earlier age.

One of the things that older couples often remark on, when they take part in relationship surveys, is that the sex just gets 'better and better' with time. That the red hot passion of their early years has been replaced by sex enveloped with love and caring, and that the whole experience is somehow deeper and richer. Obviously, they have found a way to completely lower their Heart Protectors, so that they can embrace each other at a deep and profound level. With these relationships, each individual has learnt to fully open while in the presence of another human being, who loves and supports them. But that is definitely *not* what happens when a teenager is masturbating over a sexual image on a computer screen.

Now this is not meant to turn this discussion into a moral crusade, arguing that online pornography, or any pornography is evil, and should be banned (and while we're about it, masturbation is also evil because it makes you go blind). No, that is not it at all. But what I have come to believe is that there are emotional and energetic consequences to pornography, if engaged in from too early an age, or over a sustained period of time, or where sex is completely divorced from any positive emotional context.

Yes, if someone has sex while looking at online sexual images, the Heart Protector is open. It has to be, because sexual desire is involved.But, in addition, if the Heart Protector is open, it also allows energy and information to flood into the individual's Heart space. But in the absence of a 'flesh and bone' human being on the other end of the sexual interaction, the only messages which can enter this individual's Heart Space are the wrong ones, and they will lack any emotional connection and closeness. The only definite things they are learning is about how to fantasize and how to get their rocks off.

Unfortunately, over time, the teenager starts to dissociate sexual activity from any kind of emotional contact, and the pornographic sex act becomes cold and dry and controlled, and not the warm and wet and unpredictable sort you get when you throw another human being into the equation.

The sexual psychologist, Dr Michael Bader, in his book *Arousal: The Secret Logic of Sexual Fantasies*, believes that for sex to be truly fulfilling it needs to contain an equal element of *selfishness* and *selflessness*. We need to get our own needs fulfilled, while at the same time being sensitive and ensuring that our partner's needs are fulfilled as well.

This may be one reason why the majority of women don't get turned on by male orientated pornography... because of the lack of real emotional connection between the individuals involved.

If you were to put this into astrological terms, it would equate to needing to keep both selfish Aries and selfless Libra happy at the same time.

We have already seen that, according to Attachment theory, deep down, human beings long for an emotional connection and closeness with at least one other human being. This is a deep seated need within us, and our continued happiness is therefore dependent upon forming at least one close emotional connection with another person. But when it is just you and a computer screen (or laptop, or tablet, or mobile), there is no one else who can tell you to 'move just a little bit to the left'. So the practical skills of emotional empathy, intimacy, and communication are never developed within a sexual context.

And as fear of true intimacy grows, the only time when the Heart Protector can be open is when they are sat in front of their computer, surfing. So it is all Aries (my needs) and no Libra (the needs of the other person), and there is no possibility of developing emotional closeness and the skills required to support and enhance it. This means that whenever such an individual ever attempts to form a real, emotional relationship with another human being, then they will be faced with a stark dilemma. Either work through their fears around intimacy within the context of a real and messy relationship... Or dump the relationship, and run back to the safety of their computer and predictable fantasy world.

Although they may find their online world deeply frustrating, because we all crave emotional connection, which online pornography can never provide, there is now strong evidence that many people today have become trapped in a cage from which they cannot escape, a cage of their own making, and this is distorting the relationships between many young men and women, turning their budding relationships toxic.

Because sex is such a fundamental and powerful human drive, it cannot be avoided, even in a monastery. For many, the only way they experience sex now, while feeling safe and secure, is through online pornography, which they return to time and time again, because the possibility of true intimacy is perceived as too risky, too unpredictable. For such people, healing the Heart Protector meridian is essential.

Finally, it is important for us to be able to 'open' our Heart Protector meridian, from time to time, because it is the difference between having an 'open' or 'closed' mind.

The cognitive psychologist Dr Carol S. Dweck, has been studying whether some beliefs are harder to shift than others, and so whether some people are more open to persuasion. In her book *Mindset: How You Can Fulfil Your Potential*, she writes about her discoveries.

According to Dweck, there are two types of mindset. The first she refers to as *fixed*, and these belong to people who stubbornly 'do things their way', who are wary of stepping outside their comfort zones, who see effort and growth in negative terms, and who are averse to being stretched.

The second mindset she refers to as 'growth' mindsets, and these belong to people who are more mentally open and flexible, more amenable to learning, more open to the prospect of change and challenge, and they prefer, unlike those with a fixed mindset, to listen to and assimilate the viewpoints of others.

Some of us, it seems, are genuinely open to influence. Others just want to be 'right' without bothering to first check that our beliefs do indeed fit the facts of a particular situation.

In the final analysis, whether you allow your Heart Protector to be open or closed also depends on how you want to live your life, the sort of person you want to be, and kind of the belief-set around which you want to build your life. But if you want to be open to new ideas, then you will eventually need to let your Heart Protector guard down, at some point, to allow them 'in'. Otherwise, they have no chance of taking root.

Layouts for healing the Heart Protector meridian:

I will now outline a simple process which can help to re-align and re-train the Heart Protector meridian.

It can be used in relation to a single individual or a group of people, or a company or organisation, or even a recurring situation... whenever or wherever you feel your Heart is either too open or too closed.

The Crystal Quality layout for this process uses the following:

A =Pyrite
B =Golden Beryl
C =Mahogany Obsidian
D =Blue Angelite

This layout is also available to work with as an Audio Essence.

In these are laid out around the physical body in the pattern shown below:

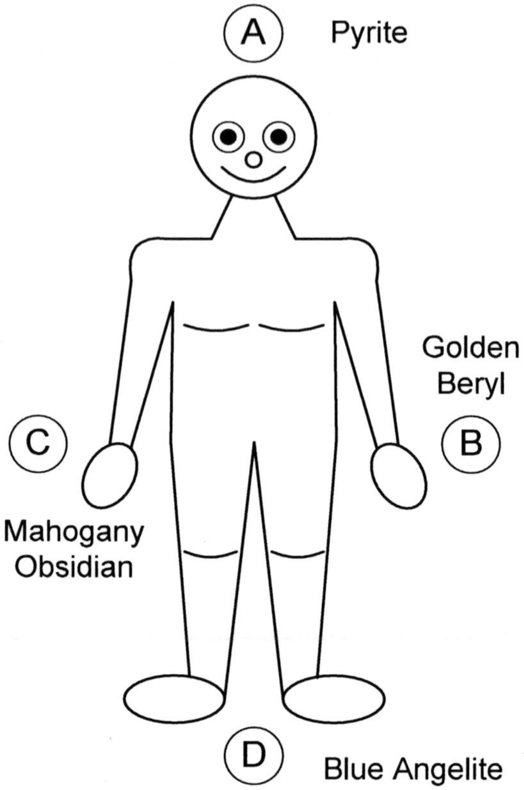

Figure 4: Heart Protector Meridian Layout

To open the Heart Protector meridian a Hessonite Garnet is placed on the Brow chakra, and to close it a Cobalto-Calcite is placed on the Brow chakra.

The process to re-train the Heart Protector is as follows:

> Step 1: Place the Crystal Quality layout around your physical body.
>
> Step 2: Bring to mind the individual, situation, group of people,

or organisation which you wish to re-align your Heart Protector towards.

Step 3: If you wish to **open** your Heart Protector meridian, then place a Hessonite Garnet on your Brow chakra, visualise the person(s), and continue to repeat the following phrase:

I open my heart to <XXX> when they have my best interests at heart, and I renounce the past between myself and <XXX>.

Alternatively: If you wish to **close** your Heart Protector meridian, then place a Cobalto-Calcite on your Brow chakra, visualise the person(s), and continue to repeat the following phrase:

I close my heart to <XXX> when they no longer have my best interests at heart, and I renounce the past between myself and <XXX>.

Step 4: Continue until complete.

Before you commence this process, dowse or muscle test to discover how long to continue the process for, or repeat the process for at least 5 minutes if dowsing / muscle testing is not a viable option.

You may need to repeat this process everyday over 10 to 15 days before your unconscious mind is completely re-aligned to the new set-up. You can also repeat this process as a 'top-up' before meeting this person(s) in real-life... and you may choose to repeat the words 'silently' while in their presence to help strengthen your unconscious resolve.

The Heart Protector meridian is linked to the astrological sign of Libra, and is very much associated with holding on to the past, which is why it helps to affirm that you are renouncing the past between you and the other person.

In addition, because there may even be times when you need to 'close' your Heart Protector to family and friends, and even times when you want to be 'open' to someone who you are normally completely closed to, the intention statement also includes the qualification about their 'having your best interests at heart'. This requires that your Heart Protector meridian first scans the other person and decide whether it is OK to open to them or not.

The objective of this process is not to retrain your Heart Protector so that it is either completely open or welded shut, but to reintroduce a degree of intelligence and flexibility towards this other person, so that your Heart Protector meridian can appropriately respond to the situation in which you find yourself.

Important: If someone has experienced deep and sustained abuse, that has harmed their Heart Protector meridian, it is almost certain they will need prolonged therapy and emotional healing from a trained energy worker, counsellor or psychologist. Although the above techniques can help, if at all possible, any person in need of such healing should seek out a qualified professional. For such situations, there is usually a lot of other emotional stuff going on beneath the surface, and you will need a qualified individual to help you work through it all.

<u>Final Thoughts</u>:

Our Heart Space is not only influenced by the people around us, but it is also heavily influenced by what we read and what we watch.

So an interesting experiment to try is to read a newspaper, or watch the evening news, with your Heart Protector meridian open... and then again with it closed... and see how this changes your experience, see if this changes the way that you react emotionally to what you read and what you watch.

C6. Practical Paul Brunton:

Paul Brunton (1898 to 1981) was a philosopher, mystic and world traveller, who started his career as a journalist, but eventually went on to write about the yogis, mystics and holy men he encountered during his many trips abroad.

His books include *A Search in Hidden India, The Secret Path, A Search in Secret Egypt,* and *A Hermit in the Himalayas.* He is also known for introducing Eastern spiritual thought and practices to a wider Western readership, and also bringing the West's attention to the teachings of the enlightened master Ramana Maharishi.

According to Paul Brunton, if someone seriously felt that they were under psychic attack, then they should immediately do the following three practical things:

- Turn on all the lights
- Take a cold shower
- Read or watch something funny

Personally, I have always liked this advice, because it is simple, practical and, for the majority of people, easily achievable. But why does Paul Brunton zero in on these three activities in particular?

<u>Turn on all the lights</u>:

In esoteric Chinese thought, there is a belief that beings of a low vibration find it difficult to function where there is bright light, and so the more lights you turn on, the more it harms them. But you could also argue that the human brain prefers light to darkness, and so the more lights you have on, the safer your brain / personality will feel. This makes sense, because when it is dark, you are at a major disadvantage, you cannot see if any predator is about to attack you, it is just too dark to see. When there is light, your eyes can function correctly, and so your brain feels safe.

The only thing I would add to this is the difference between physical light, which is generated from normal light-bulbs (or the Sun), and subtle light, which is generated by crystals, particularly clear quartz. If you therefore want to create a spiritually illuminated space, having a few large clear quartz crystals or clusters around the room, especially in the corners of the room, will help to achieve this.

To stay effective, the crystals will need to be cleansed on a regular basis, and some of these large single crystals or clusters are quite expensive, which may practically limit what you can achieve. Information on how to cleanse crystals can be found in my free ebook *Samarpan Alchemy Supplementary Manual* (refer to Appendix D).

However, if purchasing large clear quartz crystals is not a viable option for you, then try using sound instead of light. Purchase a CD of spiritual sounds, such as Gregorian chants or Tibetan mantras, and play whenever you need to bring more 'light' into your home space.

<u>Take a cold shower</u>:

If you take a cold shower, then this creates an immediate reaction in your physical body, causing it to pull back / inwards, which also has the result of dislodging many energy hooks or debris that is trying to stay attached to you. It may not be effective against the more insidious energies, but for the day-to-day stuff you may pick up, it works really well. Also, since time unknown, water has always been seen as cleansing and purifying. Naturally, water creates a sense of flow, and so it is also associated with our emotions.

In many spiritual traditions, water was, and is still, seen as something which can purify us, and carry away any stuck emotions, any unwanted attachments. This is why water is used during baptism, to clear away the individual's unclean past, and to make room for their new beginning. So taking a quick cold shower, if you feel that you are under some kind of psychic influence is a good move to make (especially if you follow it up with a long, warm bath).

Fire is also an element which can be used to purify. However, you don't find many religions which attract new converts willing to undergo a baptism of fire. Strange that.

Watch something funny:

The devil, and his host of demons, is believed to hate being laughed at. So if you can switch on 'the funny' when you are feeling psychically threatened then this is a good way of countering any dodgy energies which may be trying to connect to you.

The sound of people genuinely laughing is meant to have a very high vibration. Laughter and smiles also make us feel good, it not only exercises our face muscles, but it also releases lots of healthy, positive chemicals into our brain and bloodstream.

It is therefore wise to keep a mental list of all those things that make you laugh, and make you smile – situation comedies, sketch shows, movies – anything that you can put into a DVD player to lighten and brighten your mood... and one of the advantages of YouTube is many of these clips are free and only a click away.

Classical music, especially Bach, is also meant to have a high vibration, and so can quickly raise the spiritual vibration within any given space.

According to David R. Hawkins, *The Big Blue*, a movie by the French director Luc Besson, is also meant to have a very high vibration, something I can attest too. I used to know a lady from Ireland, who introduced me to its magic once, at a cinema in Bradford in the early 1990s. When you watch it, it's as if your whole aura is being swept clean of any bad emotions or dodgy energies. I don't know how or why a mere film can do this, but for me and others, it does. So that is something else you may like to watch and try. And while you're about it, why not sit down and come up with your own list of feel-good films and shows.

In addition to Paul Brunton's top three tips for psychic protection, I would also like to add one of my own, which is often overlooked, but can also shift stuck energies quickly and towards the positive, and definitely doesn't cost a small fortune.

Spring clean and de-clutter:

Dust is a sign that air isn't flowing. It is also a sign that energy isn't flowing. Large amounts of clutter also inhibit the flow of air and of energy. The more that you clutter up your living-space, the more you will inhibit the flow of air and energy, and many esoteric traditions believe that low vibrational beings like to hang out in places where the energy is stagnant.

What is the answer?

De-clutter and have a spring clean! The more you can de-clutter your living space, the more air can circulate, the more energy can flow, and the more that space will attract even more positive energies. It sounds like a chore… but at the end of it, you'll feel a lot better… and from a Feng Shui perspective, everything you own, all your possessions, require a part of your energy to keep them in place in your life. So if you can release an object you no longer use or require, take it to a charity shop or to the re-cycling centre, then this also frees up a part of your energy, which can start to be used elsewhere. So it's a win-win situation.

C7. The Golden Shield:

There are times when big, bulky books contain very little of value, while small, thin books can be packed full with absolute diamonds and gems of wisdom.

In my humble opinion, one such 'small book of wisdom' is *Understanding Auras* by Joseph Ostrom, which was originally published back in the late 1980s.

This book is currently out of print, but if you are lucky you can still find it available via Amazon or other online second hand booksellers. It is well worth tracking down, because it is full of useful information and interesting insights, which arise from Ostrom's own knowledge and wisdom, along with his natural born ability to see the aura around the human body.

But along with all the insights and information, there is one technique which is worth the price of the book alone, worth its metaphorical weight in gold. Ostrom refers to it as the protective aura, although when I teach it I call it *The Golden Shield.*

For as Ostrom writes himself:

> *... I promised to tell you about the protective aura. I said then that it would possibly be the most important piece of information in this book. To get the most out of this life it is important to participate with a positive attitude. Positivity draws positive events and positive people to you. With a positive outlook the possibilities for attaining your highest potential can be realised. Negative thoughts, beliefs and resulting actions limit potential and draw painful situations into your life.*[1]

1 Joseph Ostrom, page 142.

Now to put the usefulness and effectiveness of the protective aura into perspective, Ostrom tells the story of how he first started to implement it within his own life.

The story goes that, as a young man, he moved from his own small town to the big city of Denver to take up a new job opportunity. Upon his arrival, he knew no one in Denver expect for one particular young woman who soon became his only friend in the city. She showed him around, introduced him to her family, he was able to live in her house while he was flat hunting, and she even sold him her car so he would have his own transport.

But despite this promising beginning, slowly, over time, the behaviour of his friend became more erratic and disturbed, and so he felt it necessary to move out of her house into this own flat as soon as possible. Because Ostrom could read auras, he could tell that she was mentally ill, and as the weeks passed, her behaviour became more bizarre and unstable, which made him fearful whenever she was around him. But fortunately he eventually found his own flat, and was able to put some distance between them.

Soon after he had moved into his new flat, two strange events occured. The first was when her father turned up, unannounced at Ostrom's flat, and warned him to stay away from his daughter. If Ostrom ever threatened her again then the father promised he would take matters into his own hands. Despite Ostrom's pleas of innocence and ignorance, the father didn't believe him, didn't want to listen, and stormed off into the night.

The second was when his female friend turned up at his flat one night, also unannounced. She was an emotional wreck, and begged to be allowed to stay the night. Ostrom reluctantly let her in, but was on edge until she left the next morning. While there, she became increasingly paranoid, claiming that Ostrom was a CIA agent who was in the pay of the Mafia, who wanted her dead.

Unfortunately, after these two incidents, Ostrom's life suddenly took a turn for the worse. He lost his new job when the company suddenly became bankcrupt, and he then began a long period of unemployment, during which he used up all his savings. The car that he had bought from his friend fell apart overnight, and when he took it back to her father to be fixed, nothing happened, he never saw the car again, and so was minus his only means of transport.

So at this point in the story, Ostrom is in a flat he cannot afford, with no furniture in the flat, no transport, unemployed, with no money to buy food... and no real friends or family in the city he can turn to for help and assistance.

And then, when things couldn't get any worse... they did. Out of the blue, his friend turned up at the flat, all sweetness and smiles, having bought him two roast-beef sandwiches, smotherd in gravy. He was so hungry at this point, that he hurriedly ate the first sandwich without thinking... and it was only when he was half-way through the second that he suddenly realised that these sandwiches had been poisoned... no prizes for guessing by whom.

Now, what I find interesting about this part of the story is that even someone who can literally read another person's auras doesn't always take notice of the warning signs when they present themselves. We all have intuition... but there are times when we really need to listen to and act on it.

In addition, reading between the lines, there was probably something deeper going on between Ostrom, the girl and the father... although exactly what that something 'was' is not clear from what is written here. Was it karmic, past-life... who knows?

However, I would feel confident waging good money on the fact that the girl obtained a kind of relief through dumping her psychic 'rubbish' on to Ostrom, which is why she was drawn back to him time and again, and why his life started to go from bad to worse long before the poisoned sandwich. Also, he was probably too open hearted, and may even have originally had a victim mentality going on, which is probably why he ignored his own intuitive warning messages.

So, when we last saw him, Ostrom had just eaten two poisoned beef sandwiches, and was writhing in agony on the kitchen floor… so what happened next? Well, he spent two days in a cold sweat, in his empty flat, too weak to move or call for help, and he believed that he was going to die. When he did finally start to feel physically better, he was still an emotional wreck, sitting alone, crying and feeling totally depressed. He felt that his life could go no lower...

Fortunately, the good part of this story was just around the corner... He remembered reading about a visualisation technique called *the protective aura*, that was purported to be so powerful that it was used by Indian fakirs to stop bullets fired from loaded guns.[2]

Because Ostrom was at such a low point in his life, he really had nothing to lose through engaging with this visualisation process... so he tried it.

In fact, over the next week, he threw himself fully into the process 100%.

It started to work almost immediately, with Ostrom feeling more positive and hopeful... and this marks the point at which his life started to transform for the better.

Ostrom has recommended and taught this same process to many people over the years, and is confident in its ability to create a shield of positivity around an individual... and when you are positive, positive people and situations start to show up in your life... and the negative start to exit, stage right.

2 Although kids, definitely **don't** try that at home!

What I find interesting is that the only place where I have ever read about the protective aura technique is in Ostrom's *Understanding Auras* book, which is strange because I have indeed found it to be both powerful and effective, and so would have expected it to be more widely known.[3] What I also find interesting is, through using this technique, Ostrom was able to forgive the girl and move on… or at least she is not mentioned again, so I assume that is what happened.

Through becoming more positive, you not only attract good things into your life, but your aura becomes repellent to those things which are negative, and which would seek to harm you… which is what the girl was trying to do to Ostrom.

I once had a powerful dream which basically suggested that life was like traveling on the London underground, or the Paris metro, or the New York subway. According to the dream, there were several routes which you could take to reach most destinations on the map, and if you missed the last train then don't worry, another train would be along in another three minutes, so you always had a chance to reach your destination within your lifetime. Apparently, the Universe isn't mean enough to only give an individual one chance at success in life. And if one route becomes blocked, then the map would soon show you a number of other routes to get around the blockage.

But since then, I have also learnt about the process of *vibrational navigation*, which also means that you are only allowed to access those Underground lines which are in resonance with your core vibration.

If your core vibration is one of fear then you only get to ride those Underground lines which are fear orientated, and if your core

---

3 Or maybe it's part of a 'secret society' thing… you only get to hear about it if you reach the 17th level of Cosmic Ascension, and so learn to master the negativity of the lower planes… Wait, if that is the case, I have just broken a major cosmic law in telling you about it. Damn! There goes my good karma rating.

vibration is anger then you only get to access to get those lines which are anger orientated. This means that you are hanging out with those people who are fearful or who like to provoke fear in others; or who are angry or who like to provoke anger in others. But if you can raise your whole vibration up a notch or three, becoming more positive, then the Universe responds, opening up whole new sections of the Underground to you, while closing off the negative ones. You get to ride on new lines and tracks along which all the cool and positive people travel.

Trust me, I know from practical experience that this works. Raise your vibration, and the painful situation around you can literally change overnight... although the raising your vibration part takes time, and so you have to be patient and do the work for real. You can't just fake it.

So when Ostrom made his weeklong Herculean effort to become more positive this had the metaphorical effect of 'changing tracks' on the great Universal underground so he was no longer on the same line as the 'bad' people who were out to get him.

There is still the question of why do 'good' people end up having to encounter 'bad' people who do them harm? Well, from what I can see, although positivity helps you lead a better and more enhanced life, it still can't erase any negative karma which an individual has on their ledger sheet. The only way they can cancel out that limiting karma is through coming into contact with the 'bad' people, and responding to whatever situation manifests with love and forgiveness... although that is often far easier said than done.

Now, the $1 million question... *'What exactly is the protective aura process?'*

According to Ostrom, the process is quite simple and is as follows:

1. Imagine all your current negative thoughts and feelings and

temporarily step away from them. For this moment, decide that you don't need them, you can step out of them, and give yourself a break.

2. Inhale a large amount of air and scream, at the top of your lungs, or silently if you are in the office or a crowded place, TIME OUT! ... and really mean it.

3. With that, take a very deep breath and hold it for the count of five, then slowly release it, letting go of any remaining tension and relax.

4. On your next inhalation, imagine your entire physical body is covered in a beautiful metallic gold foil. Gold is the ultimate protective colour in the physical realm; its reflectiveness and purity, the fact it will not tarnish, will keep all negative external energies from entering into your aura.

5. As you exhale this time, see this gold foil blowing up like a balloon, and envision it fully surrounding the outer edges of your aura.

6. Fill the interior of this safe golden cocoon with a beautiful, effervescent, rainbow light of positivity.

7. Inhale the cooling, soothing positivity and relax. Within your golden aura you are safe, protected from all external negativity.

Ostrom also states about this process that:

- This process is easy to do, and can be done anywhere, and the more you practice it the easier it becomes.

- The protective aura is great to use when someone wants to argue or pick a fight with you, and can help you to 'stay in the moment' and not fuel their fight.

However, Ostrom explains that the Golden Shield technique does have one catch.

The Golden Shield can deflect negative thoughts and energies projected at you from *outside* your aura... however, it is unable to deal with any negative thoughts and energies which originate from *inside* your aura... generated from within your own head and personality. If you start to think negative thoughts then the protective aura will shatter and come crashing down, and you will need to rebuild it all over again...

In fact, Ostrom said that in the early days of using this technique, after building his protective aura, it would remain stable for 10 minutes or so, and then he would suddenly get depressed, and his cocoon would come crashing down... and he would need to build it up all over again.[4]

But he kept on re-building it... he persevered.

And as he struggled with his own negativity, he started to notice that the time-period during which the cocoon remained stable started to become longer... and longer... and longer... and after several days he was able to 'step out' of his negativity and fears for several hours at a time. Which was an amazing revelation. He realised that he had gained control over his limiting and disempowering emotional state. From then on, his life took on a new and more positive direction, and his situation started to transform for the better.

You may be thinking to yourself, 'Why do I need to learn this technique... my life is going great.' But there is a little wisdom saying

4 Remember, traditionally vampires can only enter your home if you first give them permission, otherwise they have to stand outside your door all night, freezing. In terms of psychic defence I believe there is a lot of truth in this myth. Only it's our own doubts and fears which cause our natural defences to fail, and this allows harmful predators access to our energy field.

which I have found to be applicable to many situations, 'It is easier to learn something in the good times then it is in the bad times. But if you learn something in the good times, then it will be there for you in the bad.' So, why not have a play with it now, as an investment for the future, and maybe you'll also find out that your life can work *even better.*

Now, for those of you who have been paying particular attention, the method which Ostrom has just taught us is an *active* technique and not a *passive* one.

Basically, an active strategy requires you to 'do' something for it to remain effective, while a passive strategy does not require any 'doing', but is usually a matter of you wearing something, or putting something in your pocket. Active strategies can include physical actions, speech / mantras, or visualisations.

The main disadvantage of an active strategy is that you need to keep doing it in order for it to remain effective, while the main advantage of a passive strategy is that it will continue to work even when you are no longer conscious of it.

The main disadvantage of a passive strategy is that you will need to have acquired or purchased the objects you need, and you will also have to have them easily to hand when you need them... which may not be the case, especially when you are travelling. In contrast, the main advantage of an active strategy is that, once learnt, it is always in your head, and so you can deploy it whenever and wherever you need it.

Remember, in the beginning, Ostrom had to repeatedly re-start his protective aura process, because his own inner negativity kept crashing it, and he had to start all over again... although his desperate situation and determination meant he was prepared to keep going. Eventually his persistence paid off, and the amount of time his protective aura remained intact started to lengthen, and he began to experience the 'positive' benefits of his 'positivity'.

Now I must confess... I can be bit lazy at times, and often prefer to use a *passive* technique over an *active* one.

So one day I was wondering if there wasn't a way to turn the protective aura process from an active technique into a passive one... and that's how I discovered *The Golden Shield* crystal layout.

Golden Shield 1:

Stones:

- 3 Malachite tumblies
- 3 Citrine tumblies

Placement:

- 1 Citrine tumblie is placed above the head
- 2 Malachite tumblies on either side of the shoulders, off the body
- 2 Citrine tumblies on either side of the knees, off the body
- 1 Malachite tumblie is placed between and below the feet

Note: This technique works equally as well with natural or 'cooked' Citrine. Cooked Citrine is natural Amethyst which has been artificially heated, which is the same process that occurs in the earth to produce natural Citrine, although over a much shorter time period. Natural Citrine is usually harder to obtain, and more expensive, then cooked Citrine. However, some people prefer to only work with natural crystals, as opposed to ones which have been modified by man in some way.

The main advantages of using the 'protective aura' as a passive crystal layout, as opposed to an active visualisation are that:

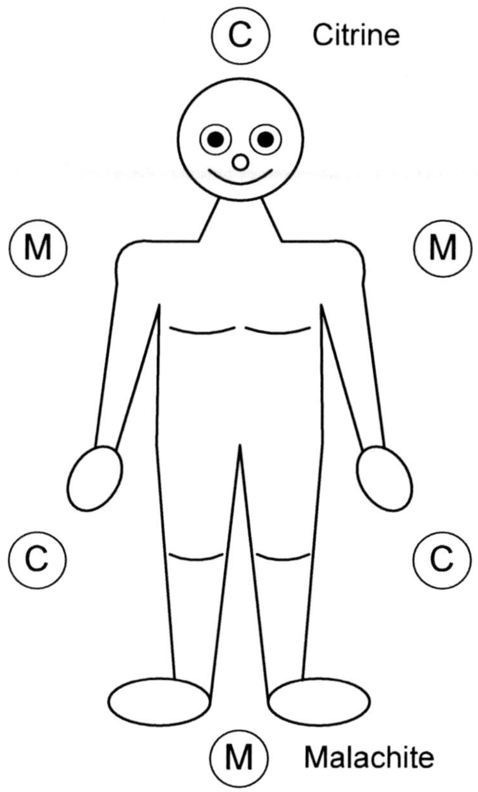

Figure 5: The Golden Shield Net

• It requires much less mental focus and effort to receive the positive benefits of this technique.

• It protects you from external negativity from other people and from your own inner negativity at the same time. The physical crystal layout will not crash due to an individual's own inner negativity, and so the individual doesn't need to continually re-create it.

- This Golden Shield layout can be worked with using crystals, or as an Audio Essence, or worn as a Crystal Hologram or Energy Card. Which means it is extremely flexible in terms of how we modern humans lead our busy lives.

- OK, there might be times when you need the full-on protective aura technique and when unfortunately you do not have the right crystals or Audio Essence with you. But if you can re-create the familiar feeling, having experienced it passively, then it is very easy for you to use it as an active process if necessary.

Golden Shield 2:

This layout is the same as Golden Shield 1, but in addition you place a Lapis Lazulli on the brow chakra, and a Rose Quartz on the Solar Plexus chakra.

The Solar Plexus chakra is the source of our lower aura, and so any negativity held within our Solar Plexus will be radiated out into our aura, creating areas of weakness, emptiness and distortion, which in turn can leave us exposed and vulnerable to negative external energies.

It's bit like a having a light bulb made of clear glass, and painting black dots on the glass. When you switch the light on, the black areas will be projected out on to the surrounding environment. If you remove the black dots then the projected light will return to normal.

Now, the Golden Shield layout (3 Malachites, 3 Citrines) holds an individual in a positive energy state, and often they can also experience the negativity / tension which exists in their Solar Plexus. Placing a Lapis Lazulli on the brow chakra, and a Rose Quartz tumblie on the Solar Plexus helps the body to gently release this negativity and stress.

The stress which is released can be general, and the individual has no conscious idea of what it is connected with, or the individual can choose to focus on an area of their life where they are experiencing negativity and limitation, so the layout will start to release the specific stress related to that issue.

The Golden Shield & Manifestation:

Occasionally, a crystal technique or layout is created with one intention, and then, when people start using it in ways you never originally dreamed of, you discover that it can also be used for something else entirely different.

The Golden Shield layout was originally created to help protect people from negativity, and enhance their own *positivity*... but I soon discovered that it could be useful in the process of *manifestation*. Remember, Ostrom was able to manifest a more positive life for himself after he started working with the process on a regular schedule.

When I run weekend energy workshops, I sometimes end with the Golden Shield technique as a way of ensuring that all the individuals in the group are in a 'safe and grounded' energy space for their return to their everyday world.

Basically, you set-up the energy of the Golden Shield in a way which includes everyone in the room, and then go around each individual member of the group in turn, asking that the whole group visualise them as being protected by a positive golden aura, an energy field which will keep them positive and safe.

Doing this proved to be very effective, and was a good way to end a weekend of deep energy work, bringing things to a safe and grounded close.

But soon people started to ask, 'I really need to manifest a new flat... a new house for me and the kids... a new, more reliable car... a new job... do you think we could include that in our end group mediation please.'

So we started to do that, asking if there was anyone in the group which needed to manifest something important... and when the Golden Shield energy was active in the room, as well as seeing that individual as safe and secure, the group also imagined them having successfully obtained the thing / situation they needed.

Although this is not a scientifically proven result, I estimate that around 80% of the energy requests, made during this group process, actually manifested in that individuals life (i.e. the new flat, house, car, job).

Now, part of this success was probably due to the power of the group. But I can't help but think that creating a positive energy space, one which can overcome an individual's own inner doubts and fears, can help accelerate the manifestation process.

<u>Final Thoughts</u>:

Positivity is very similar to optimism, which is generally a good thing. However, it has been found that the best kind of positivity and optimism, although it hopes for the best to manifest, doesn't set rigid goals and timescales.

When asked what kind of American prisoners faired the worse in Vietcong prisons during the Vietnam war, Admiral James Stockdale replied, 'Oh, that's easy. The optimists.'

Apparently, the Pollyanna optimists who said to themselves and others 'We'll be out by Christmas' or 'We'll be home by Thanksgiving' were only setting themselves up for a broken heart when their optimistic thinking didn't come true (and they had to live with their feelings of guilt that they had also let their fellow inmates down). They tended not to survive.

According to Admiral Stockdale, '*This is a very important lesson. You must never confuse faith that you will prevail in the end – which you can never afford to lose – with discipline to confront the most brutal facts of your current reality, whatever that may be.*'[5]

So your best bet is to be *realistically optimistic*, or maybe *pragmatically positive.*

I have found this to be true in regards to the tricky and difficult situations which have occurred in my own life. It is best to think to yourself 'I am going to get out of this eventually... even though currently I can't see how or when. But I have faith that I will eventually prevail.'

Also, in their book *The Power of Negative Emotion: How Anger, Guilt and Self-Doubt are Essential to Success and Fulfilment*, Todd Kashdan and Robert Biswas-Diener state that it is self-defeating to try and live in a positive state of happiness 24/7... and it is probably impossible anyway. A little rain will fall into every life, and some rain is more toxic than most... but it is how we deal with it all that counts.

According to Kashdan and Biswar-Diener, all 'negative' emotions are designed to teach us *something useful.*

Guilt can show us when we have behaved badly, fear can warn us of danger, and anger can help us identify when someone has invaded and trampled all over our personal 'space'. They all provide us with useful information, and also the energy to fight back if needed.

So when you are in the positive state, you shouldn't try to squash or banish any of these limiting feelings. Instead, you should allow

5 Ben Sherwood, pages 41 to 42.

them to arise, acknowledge and recognise them, learn from them, act on them if necessary, and then let them go, returning to your baseline of positivity. Basically, anger, guilt, and fear are places it is OK to visit from time to time, but you really wouldn't want to live there permanently.

Maintaining a state of positivity doesn't mean that you will *never* experience limiting emotions ever again, after all you are human, but it does mean that you will not get trapped into living your life under a cloud of fear or anger.

Finally, one of the conclusions of modern psychology is that an individual's conscious willpower is actually quite weak, especially when it goes up against the willpower of the unconscious mind.

Conscious will power can last a couple of hours at best, but then it becomes exhausted, allowing our unconscious habits and conditioning to take control, and soon the individual is usually right back where they started.

However, from my personal experience, if a person can maintain a state of inner positivity, then this helps to strengthen the hand of our conscious willpower, which makes it easier for us to achieve our conscious dreams and goals.

It's not 100% fool proof, but it does help turn things around... as Joseph Ostrom can testify to.

C8. Knowing Your Comfort Zone:

Have you ever watched a one year old explore the world around them?

It is an interesting exercise, because it also helps explain a great deal about how adults behave and navigate their way through adulthood.

Remember, the habits and patterns which we establish in our early childhood are the ones we tend to stick with throughout the rest of our lives.

A small child's exploration of the big world around them can be broken down into two distinct phases.

The first phase begins when the child gets bored with playing beside its mother, and decides to set off and explore the exciting world which lies just beyond the horizon. So the child toddles off, for the moment putting any thought of mother and safety to one side, enticed by the prospect of all the adventure, freedom and newness that lies on the other side of the room or play-park.

But, as the child explores, at some point the thought suddenly enters his / her mind, 'Where has mother gone?', and it looks around to find her. This is the start of the second phase.

If she is still nearby, in direct line of sight, then all is well, she isn't lost, and so the child is comforted and continues to explore.

However, if she appears to be far away, or even worse, can no longer be seen or located, then the child goes into full-blown panic mode, and frantically tries to find her again.

It either runs straight back to mother, or makes so much noise so that the mother is alerted to his / her plight, and so comes to the rescue.

Either way, the child returns to mother, and so feels safe and secure. Panic over. Until... it gets bored... starts to wander off in search of newness and excitement... and the whole cycle repeats once again.

So the repeating pattern is fuelled by boredom and the need for excitement on one side, and anxiety and the need for security on the other side.

What is important for all of us adults is to realise is that we do *exactly* the same thing. We repeat the same pattern in our lives, but often we do not even realise that this is what we're doing.

The point at which the child realises that the mother is missing and starts to panic is what we can call the edge of our *comfort zone.* This is a psychological space that, while we are inside it we feel safe and secure, but when we venture outside of its apparent protection we start to experience panic and anxiety. The comfort zone that we mentally create as children we carry forwards into our adult lives.

For the child, their comfort zone is represented by the 'mother', but for adults, our comfort zones comprise a whole host of different things, both real and metaphorical, and comfort zones vary considerably from individual to individual. Comfort zones also come in different shapes and sizes, some are quite large, while others are quite small.

My comfort zone will be very different from your comfort zone, and your comfort zone will be very different to your brother or sister, or to your friends. After all, we are all unique individuals, even if we are created from repeating archetypal patterns.

Apart from the real protection which you mother / father can provide, along with any tangible skills that you acquire during your life, the remainder of your comfort zone is built from mental constructs, your own ideas and beliefs about how the world works, which may not have any real roots in objective reality. Whether these beliefs and ideas would be able to protect you, if ever put to the test, is debateable. However, their magic lies in the fact that you think they would, and so your anxiety is kept at bay.

Modern psychological techniques, the ones which actually 'do work', such as NLP or CBT, are partly designed to update your comfort zone, and give you a better set of beliefs and ideas, ones which will improve your ability to interact with your external world. Interestingly, Special Forces training is also about giving their personnel a set of attitudes and beliefs that allows them deal effectively with the situations they encounter (although their version of reality is bit more violent than yours or mine).

As an adult, whenever you step outside of your comfort zone – i.e. to learn a new skill, meet new people, or travel to a different country – then you immediately trigger a burst of anxiety. You cannot prevent this anxiety from occurring, it happens automatically whenever you cross the boundary of your comfort zone. In a sense, anxiety is a warning signal designed to alert you to the fact you are wandering into uncharted territory, and so need to pay attention. Your subconscious mind, which usually runs much of your life for you on auto-pilot, cannot help if the conscious mind decides to go any further.

But when this anxiety naturally arises, people respond in either one of two ways:

- They manage the anxiety, develop strategies to prevent it overwhelming them, and they keep moving forwards towards their goal.

- They panic, turn around, and rush back to the perceived safety and security of their comfort zone, and look for ways to justify why they have given up on obtaining their goal (and they look for something or someone to blame for defeating them).

Because once again, when we are small children, our parents and other adults either teach us a) how to successfully handle our anxiety and go after our goals, or b) how to play it safe and live within our psychological means.

Also, have you noticed that some people, when they step outside their comfort zone, or are forced outside by external circumstances, create a lot of unnecessary psychological noise and activity? This is their inner child, hoping that if they make a lot of noise, someone, mother perhaps, will come and save them. Unfortunately, for these adults, help seldom comes (because as an adult, you're meant to be able to look after yourself).

If you choose to live out your life completely encased within the security of your comfort zone, then you will learn nothing new, go nowhere unusual, and boredom will be your constant companion. But for many people, this is the lesser of two evils. When asked to choose between anxiety and boredom, unfortunately, many, many people would rather chose a life of boredom and sameness then suffer the anxiety and uncertainty of setting out along a new and different life-path.

Many people like to believe they would have the nerve to walk down 'the path less travelled', as the American poet Robert Frost writes, but how many of us would take this path if actually given the opportunity. And what if there was no path, and we had to forge a fresh one through an unknown forest, clearing a way for others to follow? How many people would be brave and happy to do that?

For many people, staying within the safety of their own comfort zone, and the collective comfort zone of their family, group, and the culture / society they are a part of, is the much safer option.

Because, and this is an important point... we don't just have one comfort zone, we also share in the collective comfort zones of all the groups we belong to, which in turn influence our own comfort zone. In fact, you could say that our individual comfort zone is also a patchwork created from all the collective comfort zones we belong to.

For example, I have my own individual comfort zone, but I also share and am plugged into to my family's comfort zone, my local community, and my country's... as well as any other company, or organisation or social group I am a member of. These all possess collective 'tribal' comfort zones, which can influence and control *my* behaviour... especially if I am not striving to be conscious of my thoughts and actions. The fact that my parents are in their mid-80s means that their comfort zones, which evolved back in the 1930s, have also been woven into my own at some level.

You can easily prove the truth of this by seeing what happens to people when they are made redundant, or thrown out of their local club, or their family / teenage gang totally ostracises them for some reason. Their world is often shaken to its core, and they are plagued by a sense of overwhelming anxiety. For many, it's the same as the child no longer being able to find the mother. Total meltdown occurs.

This is why many of us will go to great pains to stay 'acceptable' to the groups we belong to. But there are potential dangers with this strategy of social acceptance.

In politics, once you have peeled away all the political and economic 'rational' debate, often it eventually all boils down to a question of 'tribes'.

You can always tell when a debate is really about tribes / comfort zones by the amount of heightened emotional response the debate stirs up within people, and this is one of the big problems with tribal politics, and also with family dynamics... because very soon what starts out as a rational debate turns personal, and long forgotten hurts are dedeged up as supporting evidence.

When you are part of a tribe, you feel safe and secure because the tribe is meant to protect you, and you theoretically share in the collective resources of that tribe. But each tribe has its own set of beliefs, laws and customs, and to fit in, each individual needs to adhere to those beliefs, and follow the official line of behaviour... even if it goes against their own self-interests... and the calling of their heart. As long as you behave as the others believe you should, you are allowed to remain a member of the tribe. But as soon as you step out of line... as soon as you question or dare to be different... then you will be thrown out and ostracised.

To our primitive tribal ancestors this was the same as passing a death sentence... one individual surviving in the wilderness, all alone, without the security and protection of the rest of the tribe... impossible. Ostracism not only got rid of the troublemaker, but it was a warning lesson to all the other members of the tribe to behave themselves and follow the tribal party line.

So to remain within a tribe, and the protection of the tribal comfort zone, there is a trade-off which needs to be made... safety / protection / communal resources versus individual freedom and expression.

In the Ancient Greek city states, one of the worst punishments a citizen could face was 'ostracism', to be cast out of the city for a fixed period of time, or indefinitely.

But there is another potential danger with tribal and family comfort zones. Basically, the world around us doesn't stand still. Change is a constant.

History is full of examples where a group of people have banded together, established their own collective comfort zone to protect themselves and provide them with a sense of comfort and safety, created a shared set of beliefs and values that they all adhered to... and eventually the rest of the world just bypassed them, and left them behind, stranded within their out-dated collective mind-set.

The shared tribal identity provides a comfort zone for the members of that tribe, but unless the tribe is able to *update* their shared belief systems on a regular basis, to stay aligned with what is happening in the world around them... then the world has a nasty habit of eventually consigning that tribe to the 'dustbin of history'.

The ancient Maya are a classic example of this. They had a very rigid social, political, and religious system, which bound the citizens of their city-states together, and seemed to be very effective for a number of centuries. But then, due to climate change, population growth and warfare, their city-states vanished under the jungle, as the populace deserted them.

Fundamentally, the Maya were unable to change their culture / lifestyle to adapt to changing circumstances.

It wasn't just climate change and constant warfare that destroyed their civilisation, but also their inability to step outside the constraints of their collective comfort zones, and change their society to one that was more aligned to their new world.[1]

There is a force within each comfort zone that fights to maintain the status quo, no matter what horrors lurk within.

We can see this in dysfunctional families, where the collective comfort zone can only continue to function as long as everyone ignores the obvious... the elephant in the room. The father who is violent... the mother who drinks... everything feels safe and secure as long as no one brings the truth out into the light of day. Anxiety is kept at bay through ignoring reality.

This also occurs on an individual level.

1 I am sure that any individual Mayan who put their hand up and said 'Look guys, we can't go on like this, maybe we should change our system?' got quickly sacrificed to appease the local Gods.

For example, a man, in his late 40s, can see that his factory is going to eventually close down with the loss of his job, however, there is currently very little opportunities in his local area for his particular skill set.

In the time left, before the factory closes, does he:

- Retrain in a new set of skills, which employers in his area actively require?

- Look to move to another area, one where his current skill set is in demand?

- Do nothing, and hope that after the factory closes he will be able to find a job in his local area for his current skill set?

Now, putting other factors and considerations to one side, how he responds to this situation will depend greatly on how he handles anxiety in his life. His comfort zone contains his current job and skill set. To learn a new skill set, or move to a new area, will mean stepping outside of his comfort zone.

If he is someone who is good at positively dealing with anxiety then it is possible he might opt for the first or second options. However... if he is someone who actively avoids anxiety, then it is far more likely that he will opt for the third option... do nothing, and hope everything will turn out for the best. But soon as he goes for option 3 then his fate is in the hands of the Gods, and his anxiety can only kept at bay through ignoring what might happen. Unfortunately, reality catches up with everyone in the end, and sometimes we have to face our worst fears.

Once again, we need to understand that people will go to enormous lengths to avoid the feeling of anxiety, and modern psychology believes that anxiety is the root cause of much mental illness. The mind becomes so desperate to avoid feeling anxiety that it literally ties itself up in knots, which is the cause of mental imbalance.

In terms of our subtle anatomy, anxiety is associated with our Base chakra, along with fear, and in Chinese energy medicine fear is associated with our Spleen meridian. Both the Base chakra and Spleen meridian is associated with the Earth element, and so when we experience anxiety it depletes our Earth element, and ungrounds us… it literally knocks the ground out from underneath our feet.

But what then is the difference between anxiety and fear?

Well, put simply, the way I would describe it is that fear hits us *physically*, while anxiety hits us *mentally*.

When we experience fear it is our physical body that goes into overload, but with anxiety it is our mind that goes into mental overload. If you have ever had to spend time with some who is anxious, you will know that their mind is constantly thinking, but that thinking never gets them anywhere.

When we experience fear, our body just wants to run, but with anxiety, our mind goes into overdrive, trying to *think* our way out of a bad situation, even though when anxious we are in no position to think rationally about anything. Anxiety undermines our ability to think straight and realistically. But unfortunately, when you are anxious, you can't switch the mind off and all you seem to be able to do is *think*… non-stop… which can be exhausting.

And, of course, the bad news is that if someone can figure out what presses our anxiety buttons then they can use that to influence and control us. If they can make us anxious then a) not only will we automatically do anything to reduce the anxiety, but also b) we won't be thinking straight or rationally, and so we may go along with any plan the other person proposes, and c) our constant worrying makes us even more ungrounded.

If you examine how cult leaders control their members, one of the ways is to keep them in a constant state of 'anxiety'. Then they are less likely to question the orders they are given... they are much less likely to engage in rational thought at all. If the leader can also provide their group with an external enemy to worry about and focus on... then so much the better.

But now, the good news... what can we *do* practically to prevent this from happening to us?

Well, there are two things that I can practically suggest. The first is an understanding of *The Psychology of Flow*, and the second is an understanding of your *Astrological Moon sign*.

Understanding the Psychology of Flow:

The best way to expand your comfort zone, while not also being overwhelmed by a great tsunami of anxiety, is to expand it at a rate and speed where you can comfortably deal with the anxiety generated by the expansion... so that it never overwhelms you.

This advice comes from the psychologist Mihaly Csikszentmihalyi, whose lifetime's work has been the investigation of people's comfort zones, all of which helped him to formulate his influential *Psychology of Flow*.

As we saw earlier, if we stay totally within our comfort zone, then we not only experience a feeling of security but also one of boredom, because after a while we are experiencing nothing new... But if we leave our comfort zone, then not only do we experience anxiety but also potentially feelings of freedom and excitement as we encounter new information and sensations. There are forces that try to keep us within our comfort zone (security and anxiety), but there are also forces that are enticing us to leave and expand our horizons (boredom, freedom and excitement).

Now the trick, according to Csikszentmihalyi, is to move out of your comfort zone at a rate and speed that allows you to experience enough freedom and excitement to motivate you to keep going... but not enough to create sufficient anxiety to discourage or stop you in your tracks.

In addition, your comfort zone also represents the skills that you have acquired and mastered to date. So if you can use your existing skills to master new ones, it is also possible to find the balance point between boredom *and* anxiety, between security *and* excitement.

If you do all this, then you spontaneously enter a psychological state which Csikszentmihalyi refers to as *flow.*

According to Csikszentmihalyi:

> *When all a person's relevant skills are needed to cope with the challenges of a situation, that person's attention is completely absorbed by the activity. There is no excess psychic energy left over to process information about what the activity offers. All the attention is concentrated on the relevant stimuli.*
>
> *As a result, one of the universal and distinctive features of optimal experience takes place: people become so involved in what they are doing that the activity becomes spontaneous, almost automatic; they stop being aware of themselves as separate from the actions they are performing.*[2]

Csikszentmihalyi explains that when a dancer starts to dance then they often get caught up in their experience, they forget themselves, and in this forgetting they experience a state of 'flow'... a state of happiness,

2 Mihaly Csikszentmihalyi, page 53.

joy, and exhilaration. He goes on to quote similar experiences from a rock climber, a mother reading to her small daughter, a chess player... all of whom describe this feeling of flow in terms of their own activities... different contexts, but the same basic experience.

Whenever an individual is totally immersed in the flow experience, they really don't have spare mental capacity for worry and anxiety or boredom, all their concentration and mental bandwidth is taken up with an experience of being in the moment.

Csikszentmihalyi goes on to state that although the flow experience appears on the surface to be effortless, it can only be sustained through mental or physical effort, or through ability and acquired skills, and is held together through concentration and focus. This means that fear, worry or doubt can break the magic spell which sustains the 'flow' and bring us crashing back to our normal 'reality'.

The Ancient Greeks defined ecstasy as the ability to stand outside of yourself, outside of your fears, your worries, and your concerns... and if you can do that then you are automatically in a state of flow... a state of ecstasy... because for a moment you have forgotten all the things that limit you... you literally forget yourself... which in the Indian mystic tradition is known as the state of *samadhi*.

Based on Csikszentmihalyi observations:

- When we remain in our comfort zone, we cannot enter a state of flow.

- When we allow ourselves to be overwhelmed by anxiety, we cannot enter a state of flow.

- When we do not develop skills that we can enhance, master and take pride in, we cannot enter a state of flow.

To create flow, we need to be brave and venture out from our comfort zone, just as a small child bravely sets out to explore the world around them. In fact, you could argue that a child is naturally in a state of flow when they exploring and playing. It is only anxiety that crashes their party.

But, often, we adults have lost that ability to play naturally like a child, and are lousy at locating that exact balance point between boredom and anxiety, and so end up being either tipped into total boredom or total anxiety in our personal lives.

You also come across this phenomenon in large companies and organisations, especially ones that have stagnated, and need to change fast in order to survive.

Usually, a young and dynamic manager, or management consultant, is brought in to create change, to whip the organisation back into shape, and their motto is something like 'Everyone has to get out of their comfort zones if we are to survive'.

I'm going to sound a little bit cynical here, but usually the young and dynamic manager has negotiated a bonus scheme that ensures they will be rewarded no matter what happens, whether the organisation eventually succeeds or fails, and so their words about 'We're all in this together' ring a little hollow. They didn't get to the top without knowing how to look after Number 1.

Their analysis of the situation is usually quite correct, the organisation has become stuck in its ways, and everyone has to be challenged to move out of their collective comfort zones if it is to survive.

But then what happens next:

- Does the manager try to find the balance point, so that the employees can move forward with excitement and with minimal anxiety?

- Does the manager totally trash the collective comfort zone, so that all the employees are plunged into a state of uncertainty and anxiety?

Yes, you've guessed it, what's the point of being a senior manager if you can't trash something when the mood takes you...

To be fair to these senior managers, when faced with change in their own lives, they are usually very good at dealing with their own anxiety, so don't really understand how other people could be crippled by theirs. These types of manager usually end up creating the very situation that they should desperately have been trying to avoid.

As well as having to deal with all the organisational changes and new skills necessary for the organisation to survive and prosper, the employees have to do so while also wading through their collective 'sea of anxiety'. And when people are anxious, what do they do? They desperately try to hang on to their comfort zones, resist any new ideas, and this makes the whole situation worse.

Now I admit, there are times when things are so bad that a manager has no other option but to push people out of their comfort zones, and hope for the best. But I have also seen so many bad managers who, with little or no understanding of how people function, have made a bad situation worse through their pathetic attempts at social engineering.

From my own experience, those managers who do succeed in these extreme situations are usually either the inspirational, high-energy types, or managers who can establish strong inter-personal bonds with their employees... so that either way, the work-force decides that, despite their fears and anxiety, they want to follow the manager of their own free-will.

So what if you are an employee caught up in such a situation... or you are involved in any situation where someone is trying to trash your comfort zone, and you are becoming more and more anxious... what should you do?

Well, it all comes down to how good you are at controlling your own anxiety levels. If someone else has effectively blown up your comfort zone, and thrown you into the sea of anxiety, then the only person who can counter these feelings is you.

So knowing what *makes* you anxious... and knowing what reduces your anxiety... are essential skills during these anxious times.

For example, if you are someone who knows that:

- Gardening and being close to nature reduces your anxiety,
- Reading and intellectual stimulation reduces your anxiety.
- Physical fitness and training reduces your anxiety.
- Spending time with friends and family reduces your anxiety.
- Tidying and clearing clutter reduces your anxiety.

Then ensure you make time for those activities in your personal life to counter-balance any stress you are feeling in your work-life (or potentially even vice-versa... I know of one person who was so stressed at home, that they came to see work as being relaxing).

Now in the next section we will discuss some energy tools which you can use, but the most precious thing you possess is your own knowledge of yourself and what presses your buttons... what makes you anxious, what calms your anxiety. So if you ever find yourself feeling anxious, then a little self-knowledge goes a long way.

Think of your comfort zone as your castle. You can't stay inside forever, you will only get stale and bored if you try, and you may need to extend it from time to time... But it is also your primary defence against anxiety and uncertainty in this unpredictable world... and so it is worth defending.

Knowing Your Moon Sign:

Put simply, in traditional astrology, your Moon sign represents your 'comfort zone'.

It is seen as representing how you perceived your mother when you were an infant (i.e. your relationship with the archetype of the Mother *and* your relationship with your real / physical mother), along with also representing your family, your tribe, and your physical body.

It represents how successful you were at exploring the world around you as a child, and so how successful you are 'now', as an adult, in dealing with your anxiety.

It is therefore associated with the anxiety that you experience, as an adult, whenever you choose, or are forced, to leave the safety and security of your comfort zone.

However, in *Energy Astrology*, the astrological sign in which your Moon resides also shows you:

- Which negative feeling automatically *undermines* your comfort zone.

- Which positive quality automatically *strengthens* your comfort zone.

These are the negative feelings which, whenever you feel them, also help to trigger the feeling of anxiety within you. Basically, for you, the two feelings have become so inter-linked, you cannot feel 'X' without also feeling anxiety.

For example, if you have Moon in Libra, then the feeling of *regret* will also trigger the feeling of anxiety, for someone with Moon in Capricorn the trigger feeling will be *rage*, and for Moon in Pisces the trigger feeling will be *sadness*.

As you can see from the list below, Sagittarius is the odd one out, because its negative quality is *worry* as well as anxiety. So whenever a Sagittarius Moon feels anxiety, it gets double the dose.

However, the good news is that if a Moon in Sagittarius person can find a way to stabilise and transform their anxiety, then they become emotionally grounded and a very effective emotional 'operator'. But this does take some serious inner work to achieve.

Because individuals desperately try to avoid the feeling of anxiety wherever possible, they will also go out of their way to avoid these associated trigger feelings.

This means someone with Moon in Virgo will try to avoid feeling guilty, because this will trigger their feelings of anxiety, and Moon in Libra will actively avoid the feeling of regret wherever possible.

Now, in some weird and spooky way, most birth mothers are usually very good at knowing exactly which trigger feeling switches on your anxiety, and can use this to control you from a very early age.

The mother who wants their Moon in Virgo child to tidy their room will make them feel guilty... But if the child's Moon is in Leo, she will probably get angry with them, because they hate the thought of anger, and so are likely to back down and tidy their room.

Now, if our mothers can do this mind-manipulation thing on us, then the same is also true for anyone else who would seek to influence us using anxiety... until we take the power back into our own hands, and break the connection between anxiety and our trigger emotion.

So, whenever you are starting to feel anxious... for whatever reason... then all you need to do is use the Crystal Antidote that is associated with your particular Moon sign, and this will help you to reduce the associated trigger feeling.

In addition, anyone can use the Anxiety Antidote, as it is not just reserved for Moon in Sagittarius, and this can also help to reduce your levels of anxiety overall.

Moon Sign	Issue	Crystal Antidote
Moon in Aries	Fear	Amethyst Kunzite Tanzanite
Moon in Taurus	Hopelessness	Larimar Sunstone Yellow Topaz
Moon in Gemini	Unhappiness	Amazonite Emerald Blue Fluorite
Moon in Cancer	Emptiness	Amethyst Aquamarine Golden Tiger's Eye
Moon in Leo	Anger	Carnelian Moonstone Blue Sapphire
Moon in Virgo	Guilt	Charoite Citrine Malachite
Moon in Libra	Regret	Blue Kyanite Labradorite Sunstone

Moon Sign	Issue	Crystal Antidote
Moon in Scorpio	Frustration	Red Jasper Yellow Topaz Turquoise
Moon in Sagittarius	Worry / Anxiety	Amethyst Citrine Turquoise
Moon in Capricorn	Rage	Moss Agate Pietersite Red Jasper
Moon in Aquarius	Intolerance	Green Aventurine Heliodor Blue Topaz
Moon in Pisces	Sadness	Aragonite Pyrite Sodalite

Table 2: Crystal Antidotes for Moon Signs

Unfortunately, from an astrological perspective, there is a small problem with finding the sign for your natal Moon. You see the Moon travels 14 degrees during a single day, and because each zodiac sign is only 30 degrees across, it only takes the Moon under 48 hours to cross in and out of each sign. So the bad news is that unless you know your exact time of birth, then it will be impossible to identify the exact position of the Moon sign in your natal chart.

Normally, when I am trying to identify someone's Moon sign, and I don't know exactly when they were born, I set the time to Noon, find out where the Moon was located at that moment, and then look to see what signs fall seven degrees on either side of the Moon.

Occasionally, the Moon will fall right in the middle of a sign, and so there is no question of that person's Moon sign. However, when it isn't so clear cut, the good news is that on the day you were born, there are only two options possible, and if you know what those two signs are, most people are able to identify, from the issue list above, which negative quality most undermines their comfort zone, and so fuels their feelings of anxiety.

For example, if you were born on a day when the Moon was in Cancer for the first part of the day, and Leo in the second part, then your choice is between Emptiness and Anger. So is it Anger that creates anxiety within you, or a feeling of Emptiness? I have found that most people are easily able identify which trigger emotion turns on their anxiety

Although you may not know your exact time of birth, this shouldn't stop you from 'roughly' identifying your natal Moon placement, and so also identifying the associated emotional trigger for your anxiety.

If you can muscle-test, or have a friend who can do it for you, then you can also use muscle testing to identify which negative quality most weakens your comfort zone, and this then helps you identify which Crystal Antidote you need to use.

Final Thoughts:

If you don't have a Crystal Antidote to hand, or not able to easily obtain one, then you can also use the meridian affirmations developed by John Diamond, to ease feelings of anxiety.

These meridian affirmations are given in the table below.

Zodiac Moon Sign	Meridian	Affirmation
Aries Moon	Kidney	I am sexually secure. My sexual energies are balanced.

Zodiac Moon Sign	Meridian	Affirmation
Taurus Moon	Triple Warmer	I am light and buoyant. I am buoyed up with hope.
Gemini Moon	Liver	I am happy. I have good fortune. I am cheerful.
Cancer Moon	Stomach	I am content. I am tranquil.
Leo Moon	Heart	I love. I forgive. There is forgiveness in my heart.
Virgo Moon	Large Intestine	I am basically clean and good. I am worthy of being loved.
Libra Moon	Heart Protector	I renounce the past. I am relaxed. My body is relaxed. I am generous.
Scorpio Moon	Bladder	I am at peace. I am in harmony. Dissonances and conflicts within me have been resolved. I am balanced.
Sagittarius Moon	Spleen	I have faith and confidence in my future. I am secure. My future is secure.
Capricorn Moon	Gallbladder	I reach out with love. I reach out with forgiveness.
Aquarius Moon	Lung	I am humble. I am tolerant. I am modest.
Pisces Moon	Small Intestine	I am full of joy. I am jumping with joy.

Table 3: Meridian Affirmations & Moon Signs

These affirmations can be used to reduce the level of anxiety experienced by your Moon sign, through relieving the stress of your trigger emotion, and so helping to balance and harmonise the energy of the associated meridian.

I also suggest, regardless of your Moon sign, you can also use the affirmation associated with the Spleen meridian / Sagittarius to reduce your level of anxiety overall.

The great thing about using these meridian affirmations is that they are free, easy to use, and once memorised, or written down on a small piece of card and carried in your purse or wallet, can be used anytime and anywhere.

But remember, when you are repeating these affirmations, also *allow yourself to initially feel your anxiety, and don't try to suppress it... and then allow it to gently fade.* As you repeat the words, your unconscious mind will gently transform your anxiety into positive feelings... just as fresh water will clear a muddy pond of dirt if it is allowed to flow into and through the pond.

The Moon Net:

The following layout was discovered by Sue & Simon Lilly, and is included in their book *Crystal Doorways*, and is excellent for relieving stress and anxiety, and re-charging our emotional batteries.

It contains 5 Moonstone tumblies, which are usually cheap and easy to obtain.

Stones:

- 5 Moonstone tumblies

Optional:

- Dark Blue cloth as background

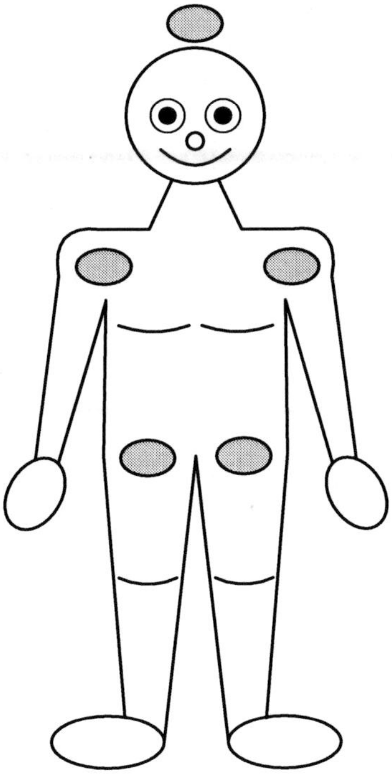

Figure 6: The Moon Net

Placement:

- 1 Moonstone tumblie is placed at the top of the head.
- 2 Moonstone tumblies are placed in the hollows where the arms join the torso.
- 2 Moonstone tumblies are placed near the hipbones.

This Crystal Net is also available as an Audio Essence.

C9. Energy Breathing:

When you were a child did you ever see for how long you could hold your breath? Perhaps you were playing on your own or perhaps you were playing with others to see who could last the longest. It's quite a normal game for children to play, exploring their physical limits.

And if you did play at holding your breath, how long could you manage?

30 seconds?

...60 seconds?

...2 minutes?

...Longer?

Now that we're all grown-up, we know that the act of breathing is under the primary control of our unconscious mind.

Your conscious mind can step in and take temporary control of the process, you can hold your breath for a short while... but eventually you will lose consciousness for lack of air, and as soon as that happens, your unconscious mind will regain control and you will start breathing again.

One of the problems with Freudian analysis is that has led the uninitiated into demonising their unconscious mind, which is often seen as working against our conscious interests and wishes. But this is not the true picture. If our unconscious mind wasn't doing all the things that only it is good at, like breathing, digesting food, fighting infection, and keeping our heart beating, we would not be alive or here now.

Breathing is far too an important function to be left totally to the control of our conscious mind. This is why it is in the primary control of our unconscious mind... which, if you stop to think about it is a *good* thing.

If breathing was left to our conscious mind, then we might get distracted, forget to breath, and soon we would be dead. Or we would need to spend all our time just focusing on our breathing that we would have no time for anything else, like eating or drinking... which means we would end up dead all over again. And we would never be able to go to sleep, and so would go crazy for lack of sleep... it would be a total nightmare.

This is why, from our first moment outside the womb to our last moment before death, breath is a constant, primarily under the control of our unconscious mind.

Now, there are three things that we need to take in from our external environment on a regular basis. These three vital substances are air, water and food. We can survive for weeks without food, a few days without water, and mere minutes without air.

Because these three are so vital to our continued existence, in fact to the existence of all life on this planet, our biology and our survival strategies are moulded around the need to procure them on a regular basis.

We capture water in lakes and reservoirs, and we grow, harvest and store food to eat at a later date. We have developed ways to prepare and cook our food to make it more appealing and tasty. We have even developed knowledge and skills around which foods are most beneficial and nutritious for us to eat.

Fortunately, however, we live on a planet with an abundance of oxygen, and we are literally surrounded by an ocean of air. So... apart from air pollution in some of the world's major cities... we never need to think much about our continued need to breathe. We don't need to first harvest or prepare the air we breathe, we just need to breathe it in.

But what has this got to do with 'energy boundaries'?

Well, the first point which I would like to make is that, although we humans like to see ourselves as being separate and unique, in reality we are totally dependent on our external world for our continued existence. Our physical bodies take in a constant flow of materials from the air, water and food we consume, and use these materials to create, maintain and repair our physical bodies.

In reality, we are all part of a vast symbiotic relationship with the plant kingdom, without which we would all be dead. The animal kingdom (which includes humans) breathes in oxygen and breathes out carbon-dioxide, while the plants breathe in the carbon-dioxide and breathe out oxygen. It's a process that has been quietly going on, every day, for a billion or so years. We also consume the plants and animals around us, and eventually our physical bodies will return to replenish the soil itself with our nutrients.

According to the poet John Dunne, 'No man is an island', and this is very true when you consider that each man is totally dependent on the world around him for the raw resources that support his continued existence.

We are not separate, we are co-dependent. We may believe ourselves to be separate and distinct because we can identify a boundary between 'us' and the 'other', but, as human beings, we rely on boundaries which are 'porous' and 'intelligent'.

For example, the lining of our lungs is designed to take in the good stuff, and keep out the bad. The same is true for our skin, and our digestive tract. All these boundaries are designed to absorb what we need, reject what would harm us, and expel any waste products.

In his book *The Biology of Belief*, Bruce Lipton discusses the major scientific revolution that has occurred over the past 20 years, as biologists slowly realised that the control mechanism for cells (i.e. the cell's 'brain') didn't just reside in the DNA at the centre of each cell, but was also located within the 'cell membrane' itself.

Not only does a healthy cell membrane allow 'in' what is beneficial, and keep 'out' what is harmful, but by doing so in an 'intelligent' way, it allows a cell to harmonize with the environment around it. As Lipton points out, we're not just programmed by our genes, but we are also being continually re-programmed by our environment, and this is a good thing, it's what evolution intended. But, once again, it means that 'No man is an island'.

But for this to work, the cell boundary has to be 'porous' and not 'impenetrable'. If it ever becomes impenetrable, then any beneficial substances, and important information, cannot cross over, and so the cell will stagnate and eventually die. It would be very easy to erect an impenetrable barrier to keep out all the bad stuff (i.e. bacteria and viruses), but in doing so you would automatically exclude entry to all the stuff you need (i.e. oxygen and proteins).

As we shall see later, this same principle is also true for our energy boundaries.

But for human beings, the most evolved and intelligent life-form ever to have evolved on Planet Earth, don't we also require other 'raw materials' to sustain us. As the Bible suggests, man cannot live by bread and water alone.

Well, physically 'No', but in terms of our emotional and mental development then 'Yes', we do need something more.

A list of other external inputs which your average human being needs in order to have a successful and fulfilled life would include:

- Mental stimulus.
- Love / relationships / emotional connections.
- Goals and challenges.
- Safety and a relatively anxiety-free environment.

For example, over the past 40 years, countless research studies have shown the vital importance of a healthy emotional bond between mother and baby for the continued physical and emotional development of the child. Any baby needs to form a strong emotional connection to its mother, and soon after birth, is looking around for its mother so that it can re-establish this 'bond'.[1]

The mother doesn't have to be the birth-mother for this process to work. If the birth-mother is not available another woman, perhaps the grandmother or a foster mother can also function successfully as a replacement. But the baby needs to bond with 'someone'.

One of the reasons behind this desperate need for emotional bonding is that the baby needs to connect with someone who will take care of it. From a survival point of view, human babies are totally defenceless and ill-equipped to deal with the world around them. They need their parents, or other adults, to step in and protect and care for them if they are to survive... and so they need to establish an emotional bond with their parents to ensure this happens.

This is one of the reasons why babies look so 'cute' and why parents fall totally in love with their children. Parental love provides the necessary motivation required to ensure the parents invest the huge amounts of time and resources needed to protect, provide for, and

1 For more information on Attachment Theory and its implications for human relationships read Dr Sue Johnson's *The Love Secret: The revolutionary new science of romantic relationships.*

raise their children.

But as the state run orphanages in the former Eastern bloc countries, uncovered back in the 1990s showed, if a child is unable to form a strong emotional and nurturing bond with another human being within the first 3 years of its life, then not only does this impact on its physical development, but the child also sustains emotional and mental damage. If the child can be 'saved' before the age of 3 years then it is possible to repair this damage, however, if the unfortunate child goes 'unsaved', then the emotional and mental damage can last a lifetime.

Even in healthy adults, this need for an emotional connection with another human being continues, and studies show that, on average, individuals lead much healthier and successful lives if they are in an emotional relationship with someone else (who doesn't need to be a romantic partner, but could be a family member, or close friend). In contrast, studies have also shown that loneliness, and being socially cut-off from other people, can have a detrimental effect on someone's health and wellbeing.

Now, we could build up a similar case for each of the other three categories on our list, mental stimulus, goals and challenges, and a safe and anxious-free environment, showing that they are all 'needs' required for successful human development.

But as Abraham Maslow showed in his famous *Hierarchy of Needs*, each higher level of need can only be successfully achieved or 'actualised' when the needs of all the lower levels have been first achieved and stabilised.

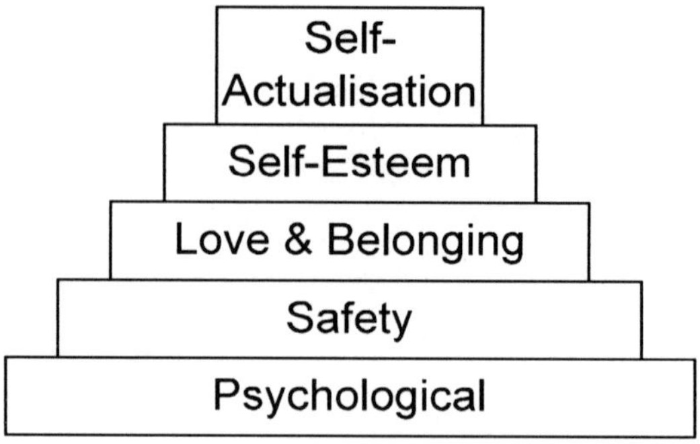

Figure 7: Maslow's Hierarchy of Needs

This is true for any individual, and it is also true for human society as a whole. Put simply, we cannot write great literature if we are feeling hungry. We cannot start a romantic relationship if we are feeling physically threatened. Our consciousness is always pulled down to the lowest level where there is an unresolved issue, an issue demanding our attention.

As one of my teachers once put it, Maslow's *Hierarchy of Needs* isn't a pyramid where you climb to the top, achieve self-actualisation / enlightenment, and then don't have to worry about anything ever again. While you are a human being, in a physical body, it is a pyramid which requires constant repairs and maintenance in order for *you* to remain comfortable and stable while sat on the top.

For example, if you have achieved a degree of self-actualisation, are sat on top of your pyramid, and then suddenly you are made redundant... then you will need to revisit one of the lower levels, address any fears and concerns about money and financial security that may suddenly arise... get yourself a new source of income perhaps, so stabilizing your pyramid... and only then can you go back up to that comfortable and stable place at the top once again.

In a sense, no one ever 'totally makes it'... we are all just 'works in progress'. We are all tightrope walkers, who have to learn to regain our balance from time to time.[2]

Up to now, we have discussed types of human 'needs' with which conventional science has no real quarrel. Indeed, many of these needs have been identified and explored using the scientific method. We are now about to explore way off the conventional, scientific track... So make sure you have your back-pack and mosquito repellent at the ready... Here goes!

According to various spiritual and esoteric traditions throughout the world, each human being is also totally dependent on subtle energy, or life-force, for their continued existence. This subtle energy goes by many different names... *prana*, *chi*, or *lung*... depending on a particular tradition. But this life-force energy is believed to be in the water we drink, the food we eat, and most importantly, in the air that we breath.

Just as a car engine cannot run without petrol, so it is believed that our energetic engine, which lies at the core of our physical body, will not run without *prana* or *chi*. It is this subtle life-force energy that sustains us, animates us, and that gives us life.

In fact, for these spiritual traditions, it wasn't just the existence of life-force energy that was important, but also its *quality*. Spiritual masters and mystics would often retreat to far-off mountain ranges, or into the silent deserts, removing themselves from the major centres of human population, because they believed that the prana or chi in these locations was pure, relatively unpolluted, and so more beneficial for

---

2 There is an argument that Buddha and other wandering sannyasins and monks achieved enlightenment without any concern for their lower needs. True... but they also experienced many struggles and torments with their lower selves along the way. Maybe their progress to the state of enlightenment would have been quicker and easier if they had also used a bit of Maslow's insight. I mean, there is torment and there is unnecessary and self-inflicted torment... Just a thought.

their spiritual development.

However, ever since the time of Descartes, Western science has had a problem with the concept of a subtle, life-giving substance or energy, and so has tended to actively dismiss it.

More recently, modern science has had to admit that the human body does produce an electro-magnetic aura, just as the ancients said it did, but scientists now argue that it is not integral to the continuation of life itself. They argue that this electromagnetic field is not used by life in any positive way, and is little more than a by-product of life, just as petrol fumes are a by-product of a car engine.

Personally, I do not believe this is correct, because there has been one scientific experiment, little known, which does indicate a) the existence of subtle energy, and b) its importance to our continued health and well-being.

The experiment is discussed in Valerie V. Hunt's book *Infinite Mind: Science of the Human Vibrations of Consciousness.*

While a professor at the Physics department at University of California (Los Angeles), her team conducted an experiment, using volunteers who were placed inside a Mu field generator.

This is a human shaped box inside which the researchers could control and manipulate the electro-magnetic field within, either increasing / decreasing the electricity present, the magnetism, or both. This is the electro-magnetic field which the volunteers would then be exposed to while they were inside the box. The researchers were even able to completely cancel out the electro-magnetic field within the Mu space entirely, which would mean the volunteers would be inside a space with *no* electro-magnetic field. However, the researchers were also able to increase the intensity of the field if they so desired, allowing the volunteers to experience a denser electro-magnetic field.

Now, if our 'physical' bodies do not use electro-magnetic fields in any positive way, as conventional science currently suggests, then being placed inside a box where electro-magnetism has been 'cancelled out' should have no detrimental effect upon us. Neither should increasing the levels of electro-magnetism above the norm have any effect either.

However, what Valerie Hunt and her research team found (a team which also included a number of individuals who could 'see' the human aura), was that when individuals were placed in the Mu box and then the electric part of the E.M. field was cancelled out:

> *The findings were amazing. When the electrical aspect of the atmosphere in the room was withdrawn, leaving less energy, the auric fields became randomly disorganised, scattered and incoherent...*
>
> *When the electromagnetism in the air was depleted, the only other electrical energy available for the subjects to interact with was the fields of other subjects in the room. As they drew upon one another's field, both fields were weakened. In the absence of an atmospheric source of electromagnetism, the interaction increased between their confused fields. At that stage general disorganisation of both fields increased. The subjects burst into tears and sobbed, an experience unlike these people had ever endured.*[3]

In addition to these discoveries, Hunt also reports that:

- The aura reader perceived that, as the room's electromagnetic field diminished, the individual's outer aura dissipated, and it was easier to see into the inner layers, which was like a 'fishnet energy' that did not correspond to the meridian system, but seemed more aligned to the connective tissue of the physical body.

---

3 Valerie V. Hunt, page 30 to 31.

• The individual within the room lost the sense of his / her own *body boundary* and *body image*. As the field within the room weakened, each individual aura reached out for another electro-magnetic field which it could use to fix and validate its own 'position'. Basically, each individual field had lost its ability to locate itself in space. However, once one aura had located another aura, the stronger one soon tried to draw upon, or cannablise, the weaker field.

• When the electromagnetic field within the room was *increased*, then people inside the room reported that their thinking became sharper, clearer, and their consciousness expanded. The reader reported that their auras were also restored, and became more vibrant and colourful.

It is possible that the human aura reader was seeing what, in Chinese energy medicine, is known as the *Jing Jin*, an energy system which lies below the level of the meridian system, and which is believed to be associated with our connective tissues. It is perceived as being the 'riverbed' for the qi of our meridian system. More about this can be found in Damo Mitchell's book *The Four Dragons: Clearing the Meridians and Awakening the Spine in Nei Gong*.

Now, I would suggest that what the these experiments directly show us is that:

1. The electro-magnetic field all around us does have a direct influence on our physical, emotional, and mental wellbeing. When we become disconnected from this field, then our ability to function is seriously impaired.

2. The origin of this electro-magnetic field is our Planet Earth itself, and so we are all dependent on the electro-magnetic atmosphere created by the planet beneath us.

3. When the electro-magnetic field falls below a certain level, an individual's aura will start reaching out to others, desperately trying to 'cannibalise their energy' in order to remain stable. This could be the mechanics behind the phenomenon of someone being a psychic or energy vampire (i.e. for some reason they cannot access the E.M. field all around them, or *believe* that they cannot, so they start 'zapping' the other people in their location).

4. Under certain conditions, an individual can lose a sense of their own body image, their distinct boundaries and so a sense of self.

5. If the electro-magnetic field within the room is increased 'above and beyond' the norm, individuals start to perform 'above and beyond' the norm, and this appears to raise their level of consciousness. This supports the idea that, according to design, position and shape it is possible to create 'sick' buildings (i.e. which make people fell unwell), and also buildings which improve and promote health and wellbeing.

But there are also interesting implications here in relation to how human beings live and group themselves together. As we have seen from Valerie Hunt's Mu Room experiment, the more the electro-magnetic field diminishes, the more strain individuals are put under, the more emotional they become, the more their clarity of thought diminishes, and the more they try to 'vamp' their neighbour as the E.M. field starts to diminish.

Let us assume, therefore, that the amount of electro-magnetic energy within any set space is limited, and let's call the measurement of this type of energy an 'E.M. unit'. So in a space the size of a football pitch, let us say, there are potentially 100 E.M. units of energy available to anyone standing in that space. But if you were then to fill that space with more and more people, you would soon discover that:

- 10 people have access to 10 E.M. units each.

- 100 people have access to 1 E.M. units each.
- 1000 people have access to 0.1 E.M. units each.
- 10,000 people have access to 0.01 E.M. units each.

As you can see, the more people you crowd into the same space, the more the E.M. units available to each individual keeps on *decreasing*... so the more people you cram into a space, the more it is likely their physical ease, their emotions and their clarity of thought will all be negatively impaired.

Now, it has long been recognised that when you put a crowd of people into a small space, they behave differently than when they are alone, or clustered together in small groups. In fact, when the size / density ratio hits a certain threshold, a 'mob mentality' can take over, and individuals lose the ability to think and act as rational, clear thinking citizens. There have been many theories put forward as to why this happens. Perhaps we can now see that maybe one potential reason is that there are not enough E.M. units to sustain rational thought for that amount of people in a set space, which means they cannot also maintain a sense of their being separate individuals.

Perhaps this explains why people in cities can sometimes be more closed off, self-centred and aggressive, in comparison to more mellow country dwellers, because there is far less electro-magnetic energy to be shared out amongst far greater numbers... and perhaps this also explains why your spiritual master and mystic prefers to meditate on top of a far off mountain... because there is less competition for limited electro-magnetic resources.

With the advent of the modern age, the amount of electro-magnetic 'pollution' being pumped out by cars, computers, fridge-freezers, mobile phones, and any other electrical device under the sun, means that not only are we fighting over what natural electro-magnetic field is still available, but the *quality* of the E.M. field is also being disrupted by our modern 'gadgets'. Less quantity and reduced quality.

But it has also been shown, through numerous research studies, that when a group of meditators come together and co-ordinate their group meditations, the crime rate in that location markedly *decreases*. Perhaps this has the opposite effect, and increases the amount of E.M. units available, or the quality of those E.M. units, or even both. So maybe it would be more helpful, and socially minded, if the spiritual masters and mystics were all to set up home in the heart of our big cities.

There is also a possible correlation to Feng Shui, the Chinese energy art of living in harmony with one's environment, and using the energy of your environment to enhance your health and wealth.

In this Chinese system, energy is meant to arise from deep within the earth, and then flow out across the land in accordance with the different types of terrain it encounters, just as water can only flow along paths dictated by the landscape. There is a whole Feng Shui tradition that sets out to read the landscape in order to identify those beneficial, positive areas to live and work.

We now know that the earth generates an electro-magnetic field, which arises from deep within the core of this planet. If we therefore assume that the energy of Feng Shui is similar to the planet's electro-magnetic field, or possibly even the same, then is it too far to assume also that a particular landscape helps to focus and channel the E.M. field in some locations so that it is stronger, and disperses and weakens it in others?

If you were to live in an area where the E.M. field was stronger then you would benefit from the excess energy. But if you were to live in an area where it was weaker then it may be to your detriment.

As well the negative effects of her Mu Room experiments, Valerie Hunt believes that the positive effects of increased electro-magnetic fields offer hope to people suffering from cerebral palsy, multiple sclerosis, and Lou Gehrig's disease, as well as emotional disturbances, sensory confusion and learning handicaps.

Now, I believe that this experiment with the Mu field was conducted back in the 1970s and 80s. At the time of writing this book, I am not aware that anyone, despite the promising results shown, has seriously taken this discovery forward to create a viable method of treatment for these conditions. As I have said, conventional science, the organisations which fund modern scientific research, seldom take the human electro-magnetic field seriously.

Now, if anyone wants to continue to doubt the scientific validity of this experiment, then I would call upon the American and Russian space programmes to back me up. Because whenever an astronaut or cosmonaut is sent into space, they are always sent with something called a *Schumann generator*, which creates an electro-magnetic field identical to the Earth's own natural E.M. field.

In the early days of space exploration it was discovered that if you sent men into space, where there is little to no background E.M. field, the astronauts and cosmonauts suffered physically, emotionally and mentally... just like the volunteers in Hunt's Mu Room. However, when spaceships started to incorporate Schumann generators in their design, which mimic the Earth's own natural electro-magnetic field, then the adverse effects disappeared.

Once again, this shows that to operate efficiently, the human body needs to be surrounded by a beneficial electromagnetic field, and it needs to be able to interact with that field. I would therefore like to refer to this interaction as a kind of **energy breathing**, which I am also suggesting is another primary human need, alongside oxygen, food and water.

Now, I had to think long and hard about whether to include Valerie

Hunt's experiment in this book. Because, even though I feel it brilliantly supports the arguments I am making, I definitely don't want to give anyone 'bad ideas'.

What do I mean by this?

Let me explain.

Back in San Diego in 2002, Martin Seligman, the father of positive psychology and the discoverer of 'learned helplessness', gave a three hour seminar in a forum organised by the U.S. government.

He was later heavily criticised for giving this seminar because the forum was organised by the CIA. The forum was on techniques to help downed pilots, Special Forces, and other 'high-value' operatives resist torture and mind-control techniques... and several of the attendees were themselves responsible for designing and implementing the United States own 'enhanced interrogation' programme.

Although he robustly denies it, Seligman was accused of helping the U.S. military design better torture and interrogation techniques, based on his knowledge of 'learned helplessness'.

My worry is that, although the Mu Room generator provides us with a better understanding of how an individual's energy interacts with the energy fields around them, and could have many positive and practical benefits... it could also have more sinister uses if this knowledge ever fell into the wrong hands.

Hopefully, you can see where I am going with this.

Now, you could argue, that those kinds of people won't be reading a book like this. But actually, you might be wrong about that. It is more likely that an intelligence officer would read this book then a doctor or 'conventional' scientist, because military intelligence tends to keep a keen eye on the personal development field to see if there is anything they can use.

When it was originally released, the movie *The Men Who Stare At Goats* was pitched as a comedy. However, if you look deeper, and also read the book by Jon Ronson on which the film was based, then you soon see there is a more sinister side to all this (and that some people would prefer you view it all as a 'big joke' because it stops you from seeing the bigger picture).

In addition, I once spent a pleasant afternoon with an intelligence officer in the British Army, who explained to me that anyone in the intelligence services is trained to have an open mind, and reject nothing out of hand. In fact, this is the key mind-set the service looks for in any potential candidate. He also explained this is why you occasionally come across intelligence officers enrolled on personal development / spiritual courses (I have met three to date, although they always politely decline when invited to take part in the group photo), because of the fact they are trained to be open-minded, and will always try something first to see if it has any positive benefits for them.

But I honestly believe the Mu Room generator experiments are so key to an understanding of how our energy system really works, that I decided that I needed to make people aware of them in this book. As you will see, many of the ideas which these experiments raised will come up, again and again, although possibly in different contexts.

When we stand back, and look at Hunt's results from the Mu Room generator, then there are two possibilities to explain what is happening:

- The human aura is generated by the physical body, and when an individual is in the Mu room that aura is dispersed.

- The human aura is generated by the Soul, which extends its energy down towards the physical body / personality self. When an individual is in the Mu room, the connection between the

Soul and physical self is broken, which is why the aura disperses.

At this moment in time, which one of these is correct... well, we'll leave that one to you and your own personal belief system. For the moment, and from the perspective of energy boundaries, it doesn't really matter which one is correct, as strong and effective energy boundaries are required whatever you choose to believe.

Now, at this point, I hope to have persuaded you that 'energy breathing' is real.

But if energy breathing is real then this raises a number of further questions:

- We all must have some kind of mechanism which allows us to breath in energy, but how does this mechanism work?

- If we have such a mechanism, then it may become blocked or damaged... so can we repair or heal it?

- If someone else is 'vamping' our energy, how can we best defend ourselves?

- If we are living in an area with low E.M. units, how can we make the best of our situation?

These are the very questions I am exploring in these *Energy Boundary* books, both theoretically and practically.

<u>Final word</u>:

I am not currently aware of anyone who has a Mu Room generator in their living room, which you could pop around and try. However, interestingly the *Awakening Your Light Body* course, created by Duane Packer and Sanaya Roman, is based on the concept of creating a light body using energy from your external environment, so creating a firm energy foundation for your exploration of higher consciousness. If you are interested in this as home-study course, then it is available to purchase and download from their website www.orindaben.com.

Many teachers also offer *Awakening Your Light Body* as a live course, taught over 3 weekends. If you prefer this option, studying alongside other students, and with a teacher who can answer your questions, then the above website will list those teachers currently operating in your country and area.[4]

Occasionally, I also offer this course in the United Kingdom, as well as many other Graduate Light Body courses. Please visit the Diary page on my website www.samarpan-alchemy.co.uk to see when my next AYLB course is running.

4 However, if you can only do home-study, please don't be discouraged. That's how I originally did it, and it worked for me!

C10. Just Run For It:

One piece of advice which you find often in personal self-defence books is, if you find yourself in a dangerous situation, then turn around and get yourself the hell out of there as easily and quickly as possible.

According to some of the world's best martial arts masters, when faced with danger, it is not a disgrace to run away. Discretion can be the better part of valour.

Often you hear it said that the true masters of any martial art are those who can disarm an opponent without ever needing to fight or raise their fist (or leg, or knee, or elbow, or whatever part of their anatomy they are choosing to fight with).

But for those who have yet to master any martial art, walking away from a potential fight is also a valid form of self-defence.

Because as Geoff Thompson writes in his book *The Art of Fighting Without Fighting*:

> *Avoidance is the very first in a long list of tactical manoeuvres aimed at 'not being there' when an attack is taking place. And it is really very simple, even obvious, but I find it is the 'simple' and 'obvious' stuff that usually gets overlooked and lands people in an affray that should never have occurred... Avoidance is being aware, understanding the enemy, understanding yourself, and understanding your environment.*[1]

1 Geoff Thompson is not only a teacher and writer, proficient in a number of different martial arts styles, but he also worked on 'the door' as a bouncer at a Northern night club for many years. It is therefore safe to say that he knows his subject from both sides – the polished theory and from raw experience.

The same principle – running away is better than engaging and fighting – also holds true in the realm of psychic self-defence. Being able to walk away from people, groups and situations that would seek to manipulate, influence or harm you is just plain common sense.

As Geoff Thompson says, the ability to 'not be there' is a valid form of self-defence, but one that also requires a skill and art that needs to be learnt.

It is a skill that requires:

- You start to listen to your own instincts and intuition, not just pay them lip service.

- You start to start to really 'read' people, and not just on a shallow / surface level.

- You start to start to 'read' yourself, and try to engage with your own unconscious needs and motivations.

- You start to evaluate your own skills and abilities, and ignore your ego when it tries to pull you into a dangerous situation that is actually way beyond you and what you can do / manage.

- You learn how to walk away 'quietly', so that people don't even realise that you have gone, and so don't try to stop you. This means you don't make a big fuss about the fact that you're leaving, and so alert them.[2]

All these things usually only come with experience, but that makes them all the more precious and valuable.

Another piece of wise advice we can import here from the wacky

2 Honestly, you would be surprised by the number of people who fail this last one. 'I'm leaving now! Don't try and stop me!'

world of the martial arts is the question...

'If you put a martial arts practitioner, who has only trained in his dojo, up against an untrained, unskilled street-fighter in a real life encounter... who would win?'

And the answer is... the street-fighter.

But that doesn't make sense. Why would the skilled martial arts guy lose? Well, the street-fighter, even though he may lack the skills and technique of the trained martial artist, is used to 'real' fighting. He is used to the adrenaline rush that kicks in during an actual fight, and so he isn't fazed by it.

Because the martial arts practitioner has only trained in his safe, predictable dojo, unfortunately he is not so well acquainted with how his body will respond in the real fight situation... and all his skills and technique will count for nothing if he can't master the chemical changes suddenly taking place in his own body.

So while the martial artist is trying to master the unfamiliar reactions taking place in his own body, trying to control his own fight / flight response, the street-fighter, who is used to the adrenaline rush, will have got in the first punch...

(And that is why you should always bet on the street-fighter, and not the martial artist.)

But what has this got to do with psychic self-defence?

Well, if you do find yourself having to defend yourself against some form of psychic attack then you need to remember that your defence skills / energy boundaries will count for nothing if you can't also control your internal response to the attack (i.e. your fear, your anger, your rage, your low self-worth, your guilt, and your 'but shouldn't I just respond with unconditional love' response).

Your opponent probably won't be experiencing *any* of this, which is what makes them so deadly and effective.

This is why, if you want to maintain effective energy boundaries, you also need to ensure that you remain grounded and centred. Any internal negative voices, which do arise from within you, you need to deal with and not ignore, because if they are left unchecked, they will undermine any techniques that you are trying to deploy.

But if you do have the opportunity to just walk away… so much the better.

Now, admittedly, there are some people from whom you can't easily distance yourself… and others where it is totally impossible. These include:

- Partners / close friends.
- Parents, brothers, sisters, close family.
- Employers / work colleagues.

With all these types of relationships and situations, they are in your life for a reason and, according to esoteric theory 'they have manifested in your life to teach you something', so you can't just ditch them and walk away, you have to find some other solution to your boundary issues.

The only caveat to this is that some people manifest in your life precisely to teach you the lesson about the need to 'walk away'. Unfortunately, people don't appear in your life with the words 'I am here to help you learn the lesson of…' tattooed across their forehead. You have to work it out for yourself. It is when handling these types of situations that many of the techniques / ideas contained in this book come into their own.

But even without using these techniques, if you analyse the situation / relationship, you may discover that you have a lot more power than you think, and you can influence how the situation / relationship plays out.

For example, a student of mine goes several times a week to visit their mother in an old people's home. Theirs is a long, fractured and convoluted relationship. The student noticed that, after about an hour of pleasantries, his mother turns from Dr Jekyll into Mr Hyde, and starts trying to lay a guilt trip on him (along with all the other emotional nasties that she doesn't want to deal with, and in the past, has just dumped on him). But now he has learnt to read the signs... and that when the transformation starts to occur is the perfect time to take a toilet break. So he gets up politely, goes to the toilet, and when he returns, he finds that this is enough to have interrupted the cycle, and his mother's psychic influence has been deflated.

I am not saying that just taking a toilet break will work for you, but hopefully this example does show you that in the majority of these situations, you are not without strategies to counter such manipulation, and they don't have to involve dropping an atomic bomb to work.

Sometimes something small can be really **big**.

C11. Psychic Groups, MBS Fairs, Therapists, Psychics & Gurus:

I have just finished watching *Cartoon Network* with my great-nephew Alexander, who is almost four years old, and one of the things which I have noticed about kids' cartoon shows, especially the ones involving superheroes with their special powers, is that it's very easy to differentiate the Good Guys from the Bad Guys.

It seems that children need to grow up with moral certainties, they need to know who the Bad Guys are, and how you can easily tell them apart from the Good Guys. They also need the Good Guys to swoop in, at the last minute, and save the day.

I suppose when you are a small kid, you're looking for some sort of evidence that you made the right decision in being born – i.e. adults are wise, the Universe is just and fair, good and right will always triumph in the end.

Unfortunately, real life isn't like a kids' cartoon show, and the Bad Guys, the ones who would seek to harm us, don't turn up in our life wearing a black hooded cloak, a twisted evil looking moustache, and with a big badge with the words 'Beware Me, I am Evil' pinned to their chest. (And adults can be stupid, the Universe doesn't always appear to be just or fair, and sometimes good guys finish last.)

When they grow up, a lot of people still carry around in their heads the simple 'good vs. bad' stereotypes, and don't realise that the world is much more complicated, and a far less black and white place then they would hope for.

In real life, the Bad Guys are most often dressed up / disguised to look like one of the Good Guys. They look handsome, wear smart clothes, brush their teeth, smile a lot, say all the right things… and so you let your defences down... and that's when they get you... because you have bought into their cover-story.

We all have our intuition / instincts to protect us, but how many times have you heard someone say 'Well, I had a strange feeling in my stomach there was something wrong about him / her, but I just ignored it and went ahead with the deal / purchase / friendship / marriage'.

There are some places and people around which those of us who are trying to walk a path of self-development and spiritual growth need to be extra wary and vigilant, because this is where we are often caught off-guard.

The places and people around who you need to keep your wits about you include:

Psychic / Self-Development Groups:

Human beings are fundamentally communal, and we most often succeed when we come together, forming groups to achieve a common goal, and this is no different when the goals are spiritual in nature.

Buddhists are taught to revere three refuges / treasures – the Buddha, his teachings, and the Sangha or community of fellow seekers.

This is a concept found in many spiritual traditions, not just Buddhism, the belief that no matter how evolved the teacher and his / her teachings, the student will reach their destination sooner if they also travel along the spiritual path in the company of a group of like-minded people.

But there is an observation made by Alice A. Bailey, in her book *Glamour: A World Problem*, which I have found to be very true in this context. She wrote that just because a group has come together to achieve an uplifting, spiritual goal, that doesn't mean that it won't *also* have to deal with and work through the petty ego-issues of all of its members. If the group isn't aware of this, then those ego-games can distort, and ultimately destroy the spiritual goals of the group (and severely burn the members in the process).

People in these situations often believe that the enlightenment and grace of their spiritual master / teacher will intervene and save them. Unfortunately, they soon learn the hard way that this isn't so.

This is true of any spiritual group, the ones that were set-up with the best of intentions, and the ones which were set-up to benefit a few 'chosen' individuals at the top.

In my own life, I have been a member of spiritual / self-development groups which have benefited my own growth immensely... but I was also a member of one group which was basically run for the energetic and financial benefit of the group leader (although you would never have guessed this from looking at their glossy website).

I didn't see this at first, because I was lost in the glamour of being part of a 'special / enlightened' group.

It is important to remember that people also join groups because they want to 'belong' and 'feel special'. If we are being honest, although we join a spiritual group because we have a deep, inner calling, on an ego level, we also like the idea of being different, more evolved than the common human herd, and fake spiritual groups and cults capitalise on this.

In the dodgy development group I belonged to, the leader had this thing that all were equal, and that no individual was more important than the group as a whole. However, I can now see that this equality never applied to them, and it was their subtle way of crushing individual dissent within the group. As George Orwell writes in *Animal Farm*, 'all men are equal, but some are more equal than others'.

Now, you do have to be careful, because one of the functions of a true spiritual / self-development group is to help us to 'put our egos into perspective'. So if you are a member of such a spiritual group don't expect your ego to be continually 'stroked'. There will be times when your views and ideas will be challenged, and your ego will probably take a knock or three. But you should be able to look back and say 'Yeah, my ego was a bit out of control back then, and I needed the knock back...'

In the hands of a Machiavellian leader, however, this process can be twisted and tortured to suit their personal needs. If someone sees something wrong within the group, an injustice, and speaks out against it, then the leader will turn this around, claiming that this is the student's ego acting up, and that they are putting themselves *above* the rest of the group. In a group where everyone is meant to be equal, trying to be different or special is the gravest sin.

The bottom line is that, if your group is genuine, then over time you will see yourself becoming more grounded, more loving, more compassionate, more self-aware, more peaceful and content, and more confident (but not necessarily in that order)... and with a bank-balance that isn't being constantly raided for little return.

If this isn't happening, and instead you find yourself falling more and more into despair and confusion, forking out more and more money to the group / leader, becoming tied up in group politics and ego-games... then it may be wise to leave... quietly... before anyone realises you've escaped.

Some groups charge money to be a member, others do not. Personally, I do not see anything wrong in charging, because in the real world everyone has to 'pay Caeser' to survive... and as a very wise Indian master once told me 'When I first came to the West I didn't charge to heal people, because the tradition in India is that healing is a gift from God, so we don't charge people.... But after coming to the West I quickly realised, people here don't value something unless they have paid for it. How weird is that?'

But the bottom-line has to remain the question 'Am I seeing a real benefit in my life from being a member of this group?'

If not, then it is probably best to leave and then find yourself a group which is more beneficial for your particular needs and path.

Mind Body Spirit Fairs:

Over recent years, there has been an explosion in the number of Psychic / MBS Fairs around the country / world.

Some are large, some are small. Some are in big cities, and some are located in green fields in the country. Some are attached to other events, such as rock / music festivals. Some are run for profit, and some are run on a shoe-string, with the intention just to break even.

But the idea behind them all is that they are events where like-minded people can come together, and experience new ideas, teachers, therapies, products etc.

And so they are packed full of highly evolved, spiritual people who are full of love and light for their fellow man...

...Oops. Did I just write that these fairs and festivals are full of highly evolved, spiritual people who are full of love and light for their fellow man?

Sorry, my mistake. Actually, no, they're not.

They are full of any person who is capable of buying an entrance ticket.

And the ability to buy an entrance ticket is no gauge or indication of the level of spiritual development of *any* human being. (I mean Buddha, with his vow of poverty, didn't carry any money on him, so they would never have let him through the entrance gate. Hitler, on the other hand, always carried a Mark or two in his pockets, so he would definitely have got in.)

And this wouldn't really be a problem... but unfortunately innocent people think that there is no danger of being zapped or vamped at an MBS Fair, because it is full of people like themselves, spiritual, evolving, people who are full of love and light for their fellow man.

Wrong.

OK, the majority of people who attend these events are decent, with their heads screwed on the right way. But these events also attract a fair degree of weirdos, whose energy is chaotic and disruptive... and psychic vampires, who have decided to eat-out for the day.

So an MBS Fair isn't the sort of place where you want to walk around, ungrounded, and energetically open and undefended. Because you don't know who you're going to meet, or what you are going to pick up around the next corner.

Just think about it for a moment. In the natural world, predators such as lions and tigers hang around the local watering hole because they know that's where all the prey animals, such as zebras, water buffalo, and gazelle have to come to drink, and generally hang out. (And don't forget the crocodiles also lurking beneath the surface of the water.) Those prey animals who drink and let their guard down while doing so are the ones who end up as lunch.

From a psychic vampire's point of view, whether they are conscious of it or not, an MBS Fair is the equivalent of an energetic watering hole.

People come there for all the right reasons, but if they wander around ungrounded and with their energy defences lowered there is every chance that they will get zapped by that pleasant-faced, smiling passer-by.

So, by all means, go to Psychic / MBS Fairs. (I still do.) They can be amazing places, where you meet amazing people.

But stay grounded, keep your wits about you, and remember, not everyone you meet will be tuned into the 'love and light' wavelength.

Therapists & Psychics:

Why do people go to see psychics / therapists?

Because they are usually experiencing pain / discomfort in some area of their life and they want to make it better, they want the pain to go away.

If they go to see a psychic, they want to know what *to do* to make it better, or they want *to know* that things will just magically get better in the future (hopefully, the sooner the better).

If they go to see an energy therapist, they want the therapist to show them how to fix themselves or, more likely, they just want the therapist to fix them without their needing to do anything themselves.

Now, what happens when we go to see a good, competent energy therapist is that they shake our energy up in some way, so that the issue we are suffering from gets dislodged, released, or disentangled from our energy body. OK, different energy therapies shake us up in different ways, but basically an internal / energy shift has to happen within us in order for the healing to occur.

Due to this energy shift, we may feel *different* for a number of days after the therapy session. Because we are so used to our energy being a certain way, when it shifts then we automatically feel different, maybe a little weird. We are not used to our energy setting up in this new way, and so it takes a few days to get used to it.

It's a bit like wearing new shoes. We're so used to wearing our old, comfortable shoes, when we first put on a new pair, we are conscious of the stiffness of the leather, and it takes a couple of days for the leather to wear in, so that we are no longer conscious of our new shoes.

So the advice for three to four days after seeing an energy therapist is, be gentle with yourself, remain grounded, drink plenty of water, and let your energy settle down into the new pattern. After that period has elapsed is usually when we start to feel better and lighter, having released the block / issue from our energy field, and true integration occurs when we have completely forgotten about the issue altogether.

But, according to Sue Lilly, this exact same process occurs whenever we go to see a competent psychic. After a psychic reading, there is also an equivalent shift in our energy field, which takes a few days to process and integrate.

So her advice is, unless it is a matter of life or death, don't make any immediate changes to your life, or important decisions, in the first few days after having a psychic reading. Be patient, let things settle down, and when they do, you will usually be able to sift through all the information you have been given, and see what is valid and works for you.

Unfortunately, that is not how a lot of people handle these situations. Usually, the majority of people try to make sense of what happened, of what they were told, immediately after the visit and often 'burn their brains out' trying to make complete and total sense of it all.

This is the wrong thing to do. It is much better to put the given information to one side, wait a couple of days, whilst allowing your unconscious mind to process the energetic shifts which have occurred. If you can allow yourself to do this, then after a few days, your unconscious mind usually presents you with a valid approach, somehow you just know what you need to do (or not).

But it is important to remember that no psychic (or therapist) has *all* the answers to our problems. A friend of mine, who is both a gifted psychic from birth, and qualified psychologist, says that on a very good day the information which she receives is probably 75% relevant to the issue at hand, and that this information is also often open to different interpretations. So the answer is in there somewhere, but you have work hard to find it.

This is why it is a good idea to stand back, wait, and let your unconscious mind work on the problem for you. Our unconscious is far better at analysing these complex / multi-dimensional problems than is our conscious mind.

So when you go to see a good psychic, remember you are not visiting an Oracle of God, where everything is 100% spot on, clear and unambiguous.

A good analogy is that you are trying to piece together a jigsaw, only you find two 1000 piece jigsaws have become mixed up together in the same box, and you only have a vague idea about what the picture on each of the jigsaws looks like (i.e. there's no picture on the lid of the box to guide you). Finally, you only have 50% to 75% of the pieces for each jigsaw, so the finished picture will not in itself be complete, so you will need to guess / interpret what the finished picture might look like.

So you start, slowly and patiently, trying to sort out one 1000 piece jigsaw from the other, putting each one together, a single piece at a time (and starting with the corners and edges first).

But this takes time, concentration, skill and patience.

Basically, this is the same approach you need to take when unravelling the true meaning behind a psychic reading.

Unfortunately, a lot of people don't have the time or patience to do that. They want an answer... No, they want THE answer right now. They don't want to have to work out the answer for themselves, they just want to be given the answer... and that is what they are paying for.

But it is this very mind-set which leaves them open to abuse and manipulation by fake psychics, or psychics who are genuine but also like having their own fan-base.

Remember, at the start of this section, we said that the reason why people go and see psychics / therapists is because they are in some kind of pain / discomfort. Well, when people are in pain it is very easy to manipulate them, especially when you sell them false hope.

The boundary issues which can occur between clients and fake psychics / therapists include:

1) Psychics and therapists who work at making you dependent on them. Because if you come back, once a week, year after year, then you have been turned into a valuable source of steady income for them. So an important thing to ask is 'With your particular approach / therapy, how long will it be before I see a real improvement from coming to see you?' OK, the human psyche is complex, and things may not proceed within the timescale that they initially quote you. But at the end of this period, you should still be able to critically gauge whether you are improving or not, and whether continuing to see them is a good idea. If the answer is 'No', then don't be afraid to stop

seeing them, and you have the perfect right to go and see another psychic / therapist if you choose.

2) In the field of spiritual / psychic healing there is a phenomenon known as 'bleeding' where, instead of the healer making the client feel better, the healer dumps all their own psychic rubbish on to the client.[1] So the healer feels better, while the client feels worse. But then the client was probably feeling bad to begin with, so they may not notice that they have taken a turn for the worse. So you need to carefully monitor if you are seeing any real improvements through continuing to visit this psychic / therapist.

3) Dodgy psychics / therapists can say something like 'Well, you are such an extreme case that it will take years, with you coming to see me every week, without fail, before you will see *any* sign of improvement. So the sooner we start, the better it will be for you.' But this is rubbish, because even if you are an extreme case, there will always be signs, no matter how small, that show your condition is gradually improving (and a competent psychic / therapist will be trained to help you identify those signs).

As a homeopath I know once explained to me, the first signs of improvement are usually mental and emotional in nature... You feel a little better, or you decide to see the world in a different way... And it's only later that the physical body improves, catching up with the rest of you.

Although some therapies produce positive change quicker than others and all individuals are different in how they respond and process this change... you should not be surprised if things don't suddenly improve, and instead evolve over a period of time.

4) Often dodgy psychics will come up with something like 'I

1 We discussed this in our earlier chapter on the *Importance of Energy Protocols.*

see something dark and evil stalking you…' which immediately sends the client into a state of fear and blind panic... and then into the waiting arms of the psychic, who is obviously the only one who can help them. Remember, even when they are dealing with difficult subjects, the issues which you may not want to face, a good psychic will always try to empower you, so that you are able to deal with these issues. In contrast, a fake psychic will try to make you afraid, so that you become even more dependent on them. So listen to the language which they are using and how it makes you feel – empowered or disempowered?

<u>Gurus</u>:

Basically, there are four types of Guru:

- A Guru who is genuinely enlightened.

- A Guru who has previously undergone a satori experience, but who has since fallen back into the state of non-enlightenment (but who may pretend to be still enlightened, a 'sort of fake it until you can re-create it' thing).

- A Guru who has not yet experienced enlightenment or satori, but who is genuine and sincere, and is following a valid spiritual path.

- A Guru who is a fake and a charlatan, and who pretends to be enlightened as a means to influence and manipulate their disciples / followers .

But as with the Bad Guys, it is very hard to tell which of the above categories your potential Guru falls into. There is no objective test, and so it usually comes down to belief, faith and inner experiences (and, believe me, just asking their disciples / followers to give you their honest opinion usually gets you nowhere).

It is possible for a disciple to have genuine boundary issues with any of the above four types of Guru, and so suffer accordingly, and just because someone is genuinely enlightened, that doesn't also mean that they are also omniscient and omnipotent... and they definitely don't have the interests of your ego at heart (urgent news flash... they're trying to destroy it!)

If you want to know more about the limitations of being enlightened, there are some interesting hints in the last section of Susan Seagal's book *Collision with the Infinite: A Life Beyond the Personal Self.*

The big problem with Gurus is that they often play the 'surrender your ego totally to me, follow my every command, and you will obtain enlightenment' card.

This is the spiritual path which Milerepa followed when he studied under the Tibetan Master Marpa. Because he had acquired so much bad karma, in order to obtain enlightenment, Marpa required Milerepa to continually build a stone tower each day, and then destroy it the next. He had to do this continually, without question. In this way, he burned off all of his bad and obstructive karma, and so obtained enlightenment.

So the 'surrender your ego to the Master' path is well known in various spiritual traditions.

The problem is... how do you know that the Master you are surrendering to is really enlightened? How do you know they aren't still tied to their own petty ego, and after you have surrendered, they won't use you as their personal puppet / slave?

There are many female Western disciples, who have surrendered themselves totally to an Indian Guru, as way of obtaining quick enlightenment, only to find themselves burning off bad karma in his bed. (There are possibly a few male disciples who fell for this pitch as well).

Although surrendering the ego is a valid spiritual path for many traditions, it isn't one which sits well with the Western mind, and wherever you are from, East or West, you need to be very careful who and what you are surrendering too.

If in doubt, don't. Surrendering to a Guru isn't the only spiritual path available, and if you are being pressured to walk down it, I suggest you run... but in the other direction.[2]

---

2 A *Creative Kinesiologist* friend of mine has also pointed out that often Gurus and spiritual teachers have their own comfort zones, and limitation 'ceilings', which they do not want their students to go beyond, or rise above, because they are afraid to face these fears themselves. This is to the detriment of their students, who are often devoted to the 'Master' and grateful for all the wisdom / experiences they have previously received while sitting at their feet. Unfortunately, sometimes you really do have to 'kill the Buddha on the road if you meet him'.

C12. Dragon Points:

The following three Dragon Points layouts are probably the most effective, and yet simplest, energy protection techniques currently found within the ICGT tool box of techniques.

The first two of these layouts were developed by Sue & Simon Lilly, while I discovered the third layout at a later date, but building upon their initial discoveries.[1]

Dragon Points are locations on the physical body which allow us to tap into a deeper level of our individual energy body, one which is not conditioned by any social and personality 'programming' which we may have received in this, or any other lifetime.

When this level of energy is accessed it always puts *your own interests first*, and so if anyone has been able to tap into your energy field, and is trying to use your energy for their own selfish reasons, your dragon energy will literally throw them out. And if they are ever able to get back into your energy field, then you simply repeat the process, and keep throwing them out until they finally get the message and realise that you're no longer a soft touch.

There is a Japanese children's TV show called *Dragonball Z Kai* where, if the heroes are able to assemble the seven magical dragonballs in one place, then they can summon the mystical, all powerful dragon, who will grant them one wish.

In a strange way, when these areas of our energy body are activated, then we can also summon the dragon energy sleeping deep within our own body, which will start to push out any alien energy intruders.

These layouts therefore help us to effectively manage the relationship

1 Before that, Dragon Points originally came from *Creative Kinesiology*.

between our own energy and the people and environment around us, and does so using our own energy.

In addition to their simplicity, Dragon Points have a number of other major advantages:

- Dragon points are exactly that, points located on the surface of our physical body, which when activated stimulate our deeper energy into action. What is important is that these points are activated, and not what you use to activate them. They are not, therefore, like crystal layouts or nets, where you need the specific crystals mentioned. With these Dragon Point layouts you can activate them with any kind of crystals or stones. You could even use pebbles which you have gathered from the beach or your garden (although you will obviously need to clean them up first). You can use drops of flower essence, or aromatherapy oil. We have even had examples of people activating the points with their hands and conscious intention when they didn't have anything else they could use.

  Personally, I prefer to use a crystal which also has associations with energy protection (my favourite is Preseli Bluestone), and also crystals which are all the same. However, I readily admit that you don't need to do that to activate this deeper energy. The activation of the points is the most important thing. So just work with what you have available at that time.

- I once heard of a therapist who took a whole weekend to remove a single energy hook from her client. Apparently, the first day involved a lot of ceremony and cleansing, while the second day included a long protective ritual before the hook itself could be 'cut'. In comparison, these Dragon Point layouts will do the same thing in a matter of minutes, and it is just as safe and integrated. In fact, many people are amazed at how quickly they complete their work, and how good it feels afterwards. Also taking a whole weekend to remove one cord is not cost effective from the client's financial point of view.

• When I first started training in crystal therapy back in the early 1990s, the talk then was of literally cutting cords with big laser wands, which were often hard and expensive to obtain. Once again, the activation of Dragon points does the same thing, more easily and for much less expense.

• With the different Dragon Point layouts you are not cutting the cord, instead you are removing it at the root... or at least your body is. As any gardener will tell you, if you cut the head off a weed it will simply grow again, but if you dig it up at the root then it has no chances of returning. The same principle holds true for energy cords and the like. Cutting them off on the surface allows them the chance to grow back again. However, these Dragon Point layouts remove them at the root, and so any chance of their becoming re-established in your aura is greatly reduced. It's as if the soil itself decides to eject the plant, root and all.

• You don't need to think about or visualise what needs to be removed, or even what needs to happen. The dragon energy, once activated, will do all this for you. It will identify what needs to be thrown out, and will set about doing so. If you are someone who has acquired many hooks and cords, the dragon energy will not remove them all in one session, because that would probably be too much of a shock to your system. But it will remove the one which is causing you the most issues first, and then, because the process is very easy to do, during later sessions, you can start to remove and release all the others.

Sue Lilly once described life as like walking on a tightrope with a long pole to help you balance. Life is basically a balancing act. Now, whenever someone else is able to hook into your energy field and drain you, it is as if they have placed a weight on one the end of this pole, thus making it a little harder for you to keep your balance. If this has happened several times, then you will have several weights hanging off either ends of your balancing pole. This means the safest way is to remove one weight at a time, because that means that each time a weight is removed you will be able to re-adjust your position safely and find a new balance point. However, if you were to remove all the weights in one go, it may feel great for a while, but it might also unbalance you completely and increase your chances of falling off the tightrope. When we sense the chance that we can finally be free of all these hooks and hindrances, then there is a part of us that wants to be free of them as soon as possible, like right *now*. However, believe me, slower is sometimes better and healthier... and when you have successfully removed the first hook your power is back with you, and so the remaining hooks are just about tidying up your energy field.

No matter how mature, qualified, experienced, evolved, or spiritual we believe ourselves to be, we all encounter boundary issues from time to time, because we are all human and live on a planet with other humans. Maintaining effective personal boundaries is part of the human condition.

But this is even more so if you are someone involved in the caring professions, such as carers, therapists, counsellors, or the medical profession, or someone who is involved with dealing with other difficult people on a daily basis – call centre personal, police, prison guards, social workers, probation officers, to name a few.

The other great thing about these Dragon Point layouts is that they are not just for emergency situations, they can also be used for regular energy 'housekeeping'.

For example, my experience of the counselling profession is that, during working hours, a great many counsellors keep their hearts and energy field open to their clients, because that is considered part of the job – being a good listener, being empathic. But being energetically open also leaves them at risk of picking up emotional debris from their clients, which they can carry back home with them into their personal life, after hours.

Just as a nurse will wash her hands on a regular basis, it is good energy hygiene for counsellors to get into the habit of clearing their energy field at the end of the day, so that they don't continue to carry 'bits' of their clients with them. And the same holds true for any profession that has to deal with difficult people, or difficult situations, on a regular basis.

I was once spent a morning with a retired fire fighter who told me that, back in the good old days, after a difficult 'call out' the team would allow themselves a brew, and spend time talking and unwinding together. It was their way of dealing with potential PSTD (all the horrific scenes they had witnessed)... although they had no such name for it back then. He said, nowadays, firemen are so rushed, and can't wait to get out of the station at the end of their shift, that they have forgotten the collective culture and comradeship which used to sustain them, which is why he believes they are more prone to PSTD and need professional counselling. I am not sure if he is right... But he does make an interesting point.

Although it is not the only way you can do this, Dragon Points is a very effective way to achieve this... and is most definitely one to consider if the counsellor (or anyone to be honest) is starting to feel emotionally burnt out.

One of the causes of emotional burn out may be that you are carrying too much debris from other people, and so need to dump the stuff which isn't yours, but which your emotional body is still trying to process as if it was yours. For example, when you pick up someone's fear your body will still try to process it as if it was your own, but will be unable to do so successfully, because it simply is not your fear, so you can never fully resolve it.

Interesting story, I was once on a flight from Dublin to the UK, sitting next to a man who was obviously terrified of flying. He talked non-stop during the 1 hour flight, and when he got off the plane he was fine, but I was a nervous wreck... And from that moment, I developed a fear of flying. OK, to cut a long story short, I tried lots of things to ditch this fear of flying... but the final thing that worked was the realisation that it wasn't *my* fear, and if it wasn't my fear then how could I fix it. It was *his* fear, the man on the plane from Dublin, and what helped to resolve the issue was sending it back to him... with love and support... but also with the firm affirmation that 'this is your fear, not mine, it doesn't belong to me, therefore you need to deal with it.' It is common to find that people are dealing with issues which are not even there's but which they have picked up from other people, families and friends, and which they just need to give back to the rightful owner. You can't eat someone else's meal for them, and in the same way, you can't resolve and clear someone else's issues.

So you really don't need to wait for an energy vampire to zap you before you start to use these Dragon Point layouts. In fact, keeping your energy field in a positive, clear and healthy state is also your first line of defence against being zapped. If your energy field is incoherent, messy and weak, the energy vampire may perceive you as an easy target, and so go in for the kill. Remember, lions always go for the easy kills first, the young, the weak or the old. They will only tackle a mature and healthy animal when they have no easy targets left.

In lightbody teaching, the human aura is described as being comprised of different layers, which can expand or contract, depending upon the mood of the individual. When the individual is happy and feels safe, then the aura is at its most expansive, and energy can easily flow throughout each section and layer of the aura.

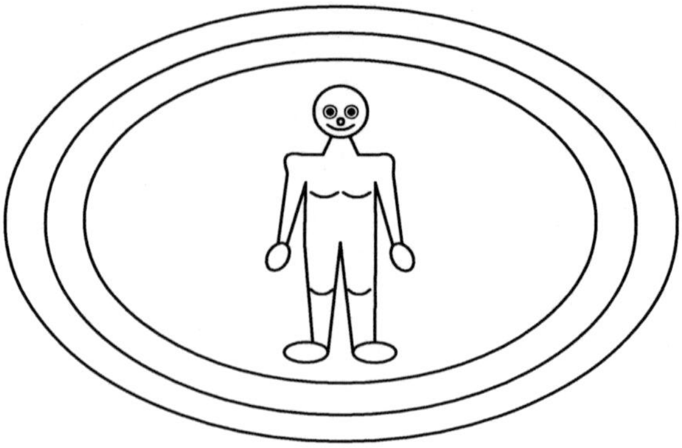

Figure 8: Human Aura – Positive & Expanded

However, when the individual is feeling unhappy or frightened, then the different layers of their aura all pull inwards, forming a more dense, protective cocoon around the physical body.

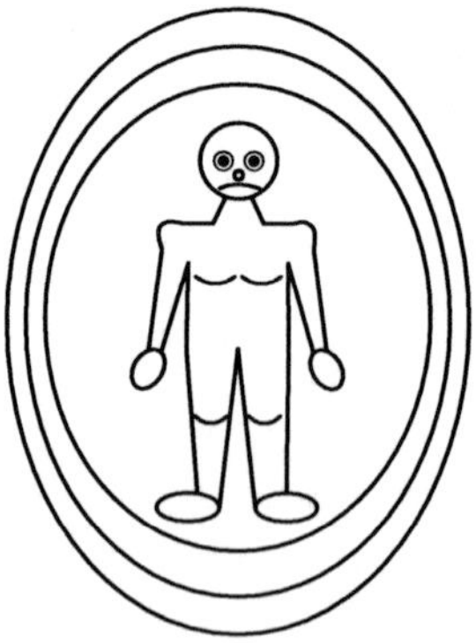

Figure 9: Human Aura – Shrunk & Protection

Now, once the danger has receded, then the aura can expand outwards once again, and the individual can return to a state of happiness and emotional flow.

However, there is a potential design flaw within our aura. When the different levels pull inwards, there is the possibility that they can become entangled, especially the emotional and mental layers, and so find it hard to separate out again and expand. If these levels are unable to separate and return to their expansive state, then they will effectively warp the aura, and also carry the memory of danger / trauma forwards on an energy level. In addition, energy cannot flow as easily within a warped aura, and so this has a knock effect on our physical, emotional and mental health.

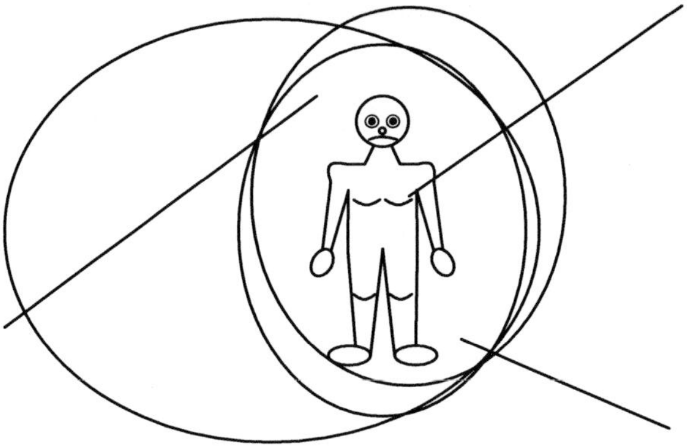

Figure 10: Human Aura – Distorted & Penetrated

But then the next problem this individual faces is that these areas become weak spots, or fault lines in their aura, which an energy vampire can use to punch through their external defences. It is usually these areas of weakness that an energy vampire exploits when trying to punch through a cord or hook to the inner levels. Because these locations also have a locked in negative emotion attached to them, it is very easy for someone else to trigger them through pushing that person's emotional buttons.

Note: In the three layout descriptions given below, I am assuming that you are using crystals of some kind. If not, if you are activating the points using some other method, please adjust the descriptions accordingly.

Dragon Point Layout 1:

With this layout all the 7 points are located on the person's back, and so they will need to lie on their front if possible.

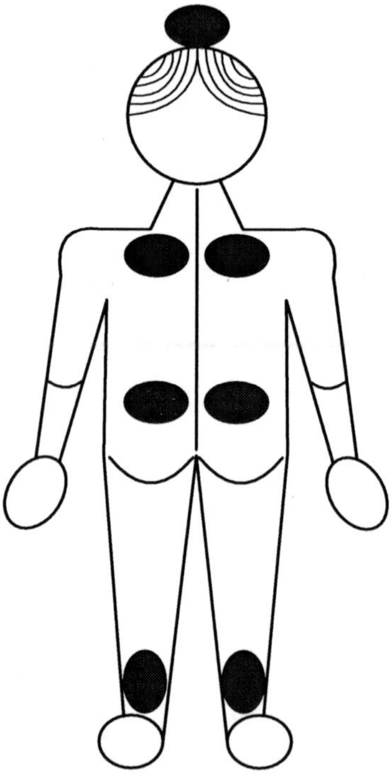

Figure 4: Dragon Points 1 – Invasive Energies – Back of Body

If this is not an option, then get them to lie on their back, and slide the crystals into place beneath them, or get them to stand up, position and hold them in place using microporous tape, and then ask them to sit, lie down or lie on their side, whatever is the most comfortable for them.

The specific points to activate are as follows:

- One stone is placed on the back of the head, or taped to the crown of the head.

- Two stones are placed at the top of the shoulders, either side of the spine.

- Two stones are placed on the back, at the level of the top of the sacrum, either side of the spine.

- One stone is placed at the back of each heel (these may need to be taped into position).

Sue & Simon Lilly write about this layout that, 'it deals with invasive energies from outside of the individual that have not yet penetrated the innermost energy levels of the body. This is useful when there have been recent or longstanding difficulties with people that are affecting stability of emotions'.[2]

This layout is useful when:

- Someone has managed to make a small tear in the aura, and so can insert a cord or hook into that hole. This layout helps to remove the hook, and initiate the process of repairing the aura.

  It is important to realise that sometimes these holes are not the result of an external, malicious act. The aura can be torn due to mechanical or chemical means. For example, according to Tibetan medicine, some kinds of surgery can cause damage to our aura, and an energy vampire can later take advantage of

2 Simon & Sue Lilly, page 104.

that tear. Also, electromagnetic pollution can so weaken the aura that it becomes prone to tearing, as can long term use of recreational / mind-altering drugs.

• When you have been on the end of a strong emotional outburst from someone else, it is similar to someone literally 'punching' your aura. And just as when your physical body is punched, although it has not been penetrated, your aura can become 'bruised', and so continue to carry the energy of the attack. This layout initiates the process of repairing the bruise.

• It is quite common to hear people say, 'It felt like I was being stabbed in the back'. Well, on an energy level, this may indeed be what happened. Although the other person hasn't left a hook or cord in place, they may have cut into your aura, leaving it torn and open. If the aura is open and exposed, the subtle energy (i.e. prana, chi, or lung) can literally leak out, so weakening us even further, and the healthy energy flow within the aura is interrupted. This layout initiates the process of repairing the cut.

<u>Dragon Point Layout 2</u>:

With this layout all the 6 points are located on the person's front, and so they will need to lie on their back if possible.

If this is not an option, get them to stand up, position and hold them in place using microporous tape, and then ask them to sit, or lie on their side, whatever is the most comfortable for them.

The specific points to activate are as follows:

• One stone is placed just above the navel and one at the base of the ribcage.

• One is placed on the top of each thigh, midway between the knee and hip.

• One is placed on the top of each ankle (these may need to be taped into place, or slid underneath a sock).

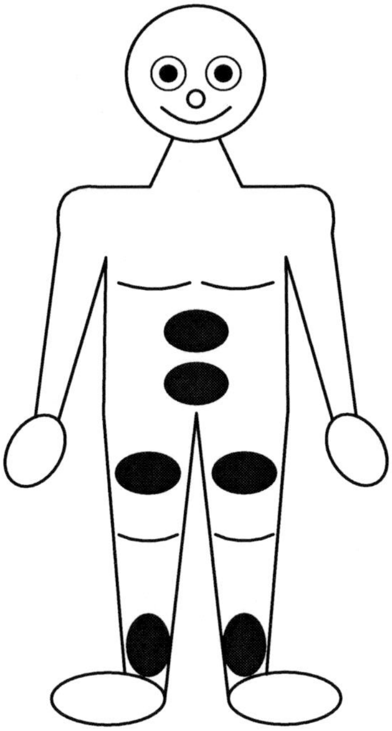

Figure 10: Dragon Points 2 – Invasive Energies Front of Body

Sue & Simon Lilly write about this layout that, 'this specific layout shifts unwanted or invasive energies that are hooked into the energy of the physical body. It is most useful in situations when other people's energies or their involvement in your life has become damaging to your well-being or progress'.[3]

---

3 Simon & Sue Lilly, page 103.

When this specific Dragon Point layout is required then:

- An energy vampire has managed to penetrate your aura, and found a way to hook into your core energy, and is able to draw upon that energy for their personnel use.

Or:

- Someone, who believes that they have your best interests at heart, has been able to access your core energy, and is able to influence you, and so get you to behave as they want... because, after all, they know what is best for you.

  This could be a specific individual, or it could also be a large institution. Remember, religion, from small cults to large, well-respected organisations, are all based on the assumption that only they know what is right behaviour, and what will finally bring an individual to true salvation. Perhaps you are born into a religious sect that condemns singing, but in your heart you love to sing and God has also given you the most amazing voice. Do you suppress your own natural gift to fit in with your religious tribe... or sing your heart out, knowing that you will be condemned as a sinner? Your position will be more precarious if this sect has got its 'hooks' into you since birth, and so you are too frightened to stand up to them and their foolish rules. But if you can remove the hooks, then you at least stand a chance of finding your own path through life.

Between the two, the intentions are different, but the effects can be the same. You are not in total control of your life, and so you are not in charge of your own destiny.

This Dragon Point layout is one to consider using when you are feeling 'trapped' by a situation, especially one which involves going up against other people, or potentially displeasing other people. It is only when we can put the whole situation into some kind of perspective, removing our fears of upsetting others, and putting aside any internal influence they may have over us, that we can discover what is right for us. It is at that point we regain our sense of freedom and ability to act.

Note: Sometimes you will need to use both Dragon Point Layouts 1 and 2 to fully clear a disruption to your energy field, and this can be done one after the other, although you will need to either intuit or dowse which one to do first. They are useful to any work being undertaken to break or transform emotional / energy ties, whether recent or longstanding.

Whenever you have removed a hook or cord, it is important to ask if anything else is required, especially if an additional energy is needed to fill the space left vacant by a hook or cord. If in doubt, then I would suggest using either Rose Quartz or Pink Tourmaline, and if you can still 'feel' on the physical body where the hook / cord was attached, either wear those crystals on that area for a few days, or wear the crystals in your pocket, and maybe visualise the colour pink infusing that area. Carnelian is another crystal to consider using... but also trust whatever crystal / stone your body feels drawn to.

For anyone who has watched *The Lord of the Rings* movie trilogy, a quick and useful visualisation is to imagine any hook or cord, once removed, melting and dissolving in the fires of the volcano Mount Doom. Just as the One Ring and its evil was totally destroyed in the fires of Mount Doom, so the metaphorical Mount Doom, which exists within our imaginations, has the power to counter any negative hook, artefact or intention. Although you will need to have watched the films for this to work. So if you ever feel that the hook is creeping back up on you... just imagine it melting in the fires of Mount Doom.

Dragon Point Layout 3:

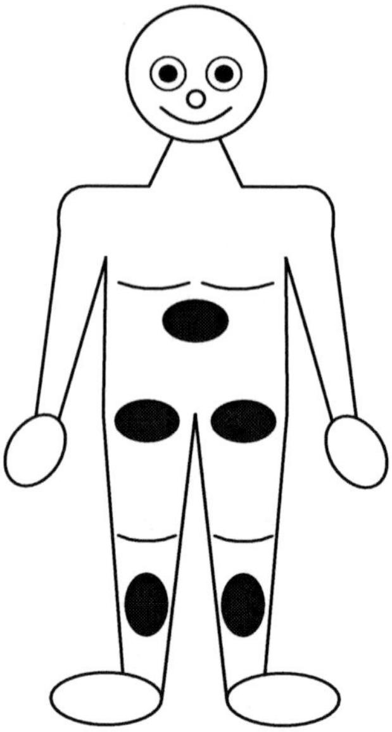

Figure 11: Dragon Points 3 – Clearing Old Vows & Promises

With this layout all the 5 points are located on the person's front, and so they will need to lie on their back if possible.

If this is not an option, get them to stand up, position and hold them in place using microporous tape, and then ask them to sit, or lie on their side, whatever is the most comfortable for them.

The specific points to activate are as follows:

- One stone is placed at the Solar Plexus chakra.
- Two stones are placed on each of the groin points, located at the top of each leg (i.e. Liver meridian points 11 – 12).

- Two stones are placed at the front of each shin bone, midway between the knee and foot (i.e. Stomach meridian points 37 – 39).

Sue & Simon Lilly write about this layout that it is, 'a useful adjunct to help support other energy work. It is worth thinking about whenever there are repeating patterns of events, or behaviour that is not helpful, or where you are aware that you have not been able to meet the commitments that you have made.'[4]

In many ways, we are defined by the promises we make, and the vows we undertake, no matter how long ago they were made, or under what circumstances.

This is made even worse if the vow was made sincerely and with a whole heart, because then a part of our unconscious mind will continue to try hold us to that vow, regardless of the circumstances, until we consciously inform it that the circumstances have changed, and it is time to let go of the vow.

For example, although the tradition has waned, back in the 1950s or earlier, it was traditional for a wife to vow to 'love, honour and obey' their husbands during their marriage ceremony. Even if she didn't mean it consciously, the vow would still have imprinted, to some degree, on her unconscious mind… and will still be running 10 years later when he has run off, after having had an affair with the local pharmacist's assistant. Consciously, she probably screams the word 'Bastard!' several times a night, cuts up his remaining suits with the kitchen carving knife, and in the spur of the moment may even poison his prize winning roses.

But, in the medium to long term, her ability to rebuild her life will be made a lot easier if she can also let go of the vow made years ago, during their marriage service. Her anger and pain won't be enough to

4 Simon & Sue Lilly, page 103.

cancel out the vow... it can only be done through conscious action or intent.

A cliché of past-life regressions is when someone, who is having problems earning money, or forming intimate relationships, tracks back to a life in a Medieval monastery or nunnery and remembers taking vows of obedience, chastity and poverty (the monastic Big Three). At the time, these vows were made with the utmost sincerity, and because there was only meant to be one life anyway, they were made to last forever... and back in the Middle Ages, belief in reincarnation was a heresy, and so most people wouldn't have even considered it as a possibility.

However, even though the lifetime and personality has changed, the vow(s) have carried over from that previous monk or nun incarnation, and so the unconscious mind does its best to ensure that the person cannot earn money, or form a 'special friendship', because to do so would be to disobey God and their sacred vows.

When we make a promise or vow, we don't tend to add the caveat that it's *for this life-time only*, or *only while this relationship lasts*, or *until circumstances change*, because we believe the relationship to be special and so want the vow to big and special too.

Many vows and promises are even made when we are not in our 'right' minds, or heavily under the influence or hormones or alcohol. But these can also have an effect, even if we wake up the next morning, thinking 'What was I on last night? I won't be doing that again.' Remember, despite what your conscious mind might think, your unconscious mind takes life far more literally, and is also not capable of lying or deception. It does what it is told, to the letter.

But then we find ourselves locked into a water-tight contract, which we consciously forget we ever made, but which our unconscious mind does remember, and has every intention of holding us to... even when our partner has run off with the pharmacist's assistant.

That is the one of the things thing which our unconscious mind is very, very good at... *remembering*.

And unfortunately the vows and promises which we make to others can seriously warp and undermine our own ability to protect ourselves. When trying to solve a murder, detectives always look to the family and close friends of the victim first, because statistics show that most murders are carried out by family and friends... they are intimate affairs, they are crimes of passion.

In a similar way, most psychic attacks and invasive energies come from people we know well, whether family, friends and close associates, and this is one of the reasons why it is so hard to protect against them, because these are the very people we are supposed to trust.

There was a crime incident highlighted on TV recently where an elderly lady, in poor health, moved to a village in Wales, and was befriended by a local neighbour, who offered to do any shopping she needed, or fetch her prescriptions from the local doctor's surgery... which is how people behave in small communities. People are good neighbours.

After a while, the lady became so trusting of this neighbour, that she gave her a key to let herself in whenever the need arose... A little later, she noticed that money was starting to mysteriously disappear from her bank account, and it was being taken out of the local cashpoint machine, in the nearby shop. But this didn't make sense, because the lady in question was too ill to even leave her own house. When the police investigated, they soon located CCTV footage from the shop of her neighbour stealing large sums of cash, after having let herself into the elderly lady's house with the key, and stealing the lady's cashpoint card on a regular basis (but she always retuned the card later on, which is why the lady didn't immediately realise what was happening).

Now, the moral of this story is that often our internal defences do not work, they do not kick in when they should, *because we trust the person involved*... they are a family member, a friend, or a work colleague... 'That's just Uncle Bert, he'd never harm me...' or 'that's Helen from accountants, she's always smiling, she's harmless'.

Human beings are programmed to be trusting of other members of our species. That is one of our strengths, that is how we have come to the dominant species on our planet. Without trust between humans there could be no co-operation, and without co-operation we would not have been unable to build our amazing social and technical civilisation. But if we accept that we must trust, then we must also accept that we will get it wrong from time to time, and end up trusting the wrong person or people. Just because someone gives you a warm smile and handshake doesn't mean that you should automatically trust them.

The question is what do we do after we have realised that we made a bad mistake and opened up to the wrong person?

Do we acknowledge it and try to repair the damage, or do we stick our head in the sands and carry on as before?

Going back to the lady in Wales, after she discovered that she had been burgled by her neighbour, did she:

- Change the locks on her front door, so her neighbour could not re-enter her house?

- Left the locks unchanged, so that her neighbour could let herself in again any time she chose?

Yes, you're right, she did what any sensible person would do... she changed the locks, so the neighbour could never again enter her house without permission. (And when her case came to trial, the neighbour was ordered to repay all the money she had stolen.)

The same holds true for any vows and promises which we may have made in the past.

This Dragon Points layout helps us to 'take back' or 'cancel' any vow or promise which we have made in the past which is no longer appropriate for who we are now, or which weaken or leave us unprotected in some way. These could include:

- I vow to love, honour and obey you…
- I promise to be your friend forever…
- I promise I will always love you, no matter what happens…
- What is mine is yours…

Once again, the great thing about this layout is that you don't need to know which vow needs to be released, or when it was made, or even how it was worded. Your unconscious mind will include all that for you. This also includes all the vows and promises which we make *to ourselves*:

- No one is ever going to hurt me again...
- I promise I am not going to be weak like my father...
- I will always protect my baby sister...
- I vow I am not going to be a failure...

But once the vow / promise is gone, you will find it much easier to maintain your energy integrity, and so protect against invasive energies and people… especially the ones which you know very well indeed. It's not that some of these vows or promises are wrong, but that they may make us too rigid in terms of life's ever changing circumstances... and we may end up judging ourselves too harshly if things don't go our way, or feel let down when others don't perform as we would want them to. For example, if we have made the vow never to be a failure, and we suffer a failure in life (which happens to everyone at some time), then we are likely to beat ourselves up for breaking our vow. It's better to have an aspiration to be a success, because this is more flexibile in terms of what life might send our way.

If you aspire to be a success then you always have the opportunity to pick yourself up off the floor and start again.

If you have given the key to your energy home to someone else, and you find that they have been abusing your energy, either take back the key from them, or change the locks... and remember that you always have the right and power to do so.

And the most important thing... is that you learn from the experience.

C13. Using Different Strategies:

Just imagine that you are living in a house with the most amazing garden. This garden has flowers and lawns, apple and cherry trees, a greenhouse full of tomatoes and cucumbers, and a large vegetable patch with runner and broad beans, beetroot, potatoes, peas and the like. It has taken you years of dedication and hard effort to get the garden into just the way you want it. People are often complimenting you on your garden, you have even won prizes, and it provides you with all the food you need. Although it has taken many years to perfect, for you this garden has been also a labour of love.

But when your back is turned... your new neighbour from next door keeps popping into your garden and *stealing your fruit and vegetables*! Although he denies it, you know it's him, because of the muddy boot prints he leaves all across your green lawn.

You have tried having a quiet word, being civilised and reasonable, but it hasn't had any effect on his behaviour. He is still coming into your garden and stealing the produce which you have worked so hard to grow. It's not as if he's poor, and he does have his own garden, which is the same size as yours, so he could grow his own vegetables if he wanted... it's just he's too lazy to put in the effort, and would rather steal from you.

What can you do?

Well let's assume that calling in the police isn't a realistic option, but you are in a position to throw money at the problem.

At first, you erect a small wooden fence to mark the boundary line between your two gardens, along with a big sign which says 'Private Property – Keep Out!' You hope that this will do the trick, and he'll get the message and stop. But the next day, you find those tell-tale muddy boot prints crossing your lawn again, and notice that someone has been picking your Brussel sprouts, cabbages and carrots.

Next, you erect a sign saying 'Beware of the Dog' which works for a while… until your neighbour realises that you don't actually have a dog, and so soon he is back to his pilfering ways. After this, you get more ambitious, and you erect a 10 foot high brick wall between your two properties, and this also works for a while… until your neighbour learns how to lean a ladder against the wall, and so climbs over the top to steal your radishes, oinions and broccoli.

Finally, you employ the services of three muscular, security guards called Pete, Doug and Phil, who together will patrol your garden 24/7 and throw out any intruders by the scruff of the neck. And that's what finally 'works'. Your neighbour can no longer feast on your home grown veggies, because he is detected as soon as he and his muddy boots step foot inside the perimeter of your garden.

Now let's say that this garden is a metaphor for your own energy field, and is filled with all the lovely qualities and juicy energies which it has taken you years to cultivate within your own energy field.

Just like the next-door neighbour, there are people who are too lazy to develop their own qualities / energies, and would rather steal from you then put in the hard effort developing themselves. If you don't defend yourself against these people, they come back again and again, ransacking your energy field, taking what they want. Often, they don't have a conscience, so reasoning with them will not work... even if you know who they are and what they are doing.

Fortunately, you actually have many different kinds of internal defences against these energy vampires.

Your best defence is your *unconscious mind* – the equivalent of three muscular, security guards called Pete, Doug and Phil – which never sleeps and can patrol your energy field 24/7, throwing out any potential psychic intruders. And because it is your own unconscious mind, it doesn't cost you anything, it works for free.

This is your best defence. But unfortunately, you may have developed thoughts and beliefs which hamper the working of your unconscious mind in this area.

For example, if we return to the metaphor of the neighbour and the garden, the security guards will work while you remain 'enraged' at your neighbour's behaviour. But if you start to feel sorry for the neighbour, or guilty about having so much while they have so little... this will have the same result as if you were to give the security guards the night off, which creates a window of opportunity which your bad neighbour can exploit.

In a similar way, your unconscious mind can protect you only if you keep your conscious mind out of the way... But as soon as you start to feel guilt, fear, shame, or low self-esteem (to name a few) then this hinders the working of your natural unconscious defences and psychic predators, on the lookout for a free lunch, will exploit your weakness. So the best thing is to work at removing any limiting beliefs or negative emotions from hindering your unconscious mind, so bringing your own defences back online.

Once again, that really is your best defence. However, in our metaphor, the gardener did try other types of defences, which did work for a while, and did make the neighbour's job of stealing harder for a time... although he did eventually find a way around them. So while you are debugging your unconscious mind of negative beliefs, it is useful to erect a strong energetic barrier around yourself, which prevents energy vampires from entering your energy field, and so buys you relief and time.

The 8 Crystal Nets listed in the next chapter can all be used to create a protective energy shield around yourself, which prevents external and invasive energy from penetrating your aura, and while you are inside, the Net also allows your own natural energy field to heal, re-assert and re-balance itself.

The 9th Net, in the subsequent chapter, gives specific protection from invasive electro-magnetic energy, and also allows the client's body to reset and re-align their natural EM field.

Invasive energy can be defined as any external energy which seeks to influence an individual contrary to their own personal will, best interests, or higher purpose, and causes their energy field to resonate in a manner which is not in harmony with their own health and well-being.

Traditionally, such invasive energies are seen as originating from energy vampires, demonic sources, or from people who are trying to consciously control and manipulate another person.

However, invasive energy can also originate:

- From people who honestly believe that the energy they are sending to the other is for their higher good (although this may prove to be untrue).

- From thoughts and beliefs directed at others from people who are unconscious that they are doing so.

- From sources which are morally neutral, such as electronic equipment, which is neither good nor bad, but which also generates a field which could take us out of alignment with our own core energy.

Traditionally, protection was seen as putting up a barrier between an individual and the invasive energy influencing them, and this is indeed one strategy which can be employed. However, recently, there has been a realisation that this is only one amongst many strategies which can be used, and it is useful to find the energy strategy appropriate for the relationship / situation.

There also has been a new paradigm entering the arena of personal growth – there is no such thing as negative energy, just energy which you cannot deal with (yet).

Therefore, these Nets allow an individual to learn a new energy strategy, a new way of dealing with energy which is non-beneficial or limiting for them. Each of these 9 Crystal Nets work in different ways, denoting the different ways it is possible to protect a person's aura from outside influence.

1. Shield
2. Invisibility
3. Transparency
4. Transformation
5. Reflection
6. Dissolving
7. Coherence
8. Perspective
9. Electromagnetic Reset

Sometimes changing the Net used will also be beneficial, as it will change the energy strategy which a person is using to protect themselves, and it will also confuse any external energies which are trying to latch on to their aura.

In addition, it is possible to carry on your person the different individual stones found in each of these Nets, to benefit from the same energy effect, as these crystals / stones work exceptionally well together.

For example:

- If a person wishes to take on the qualities of **invisibility**, then carrying Red Garnet and Labradorite together will help to cloak their aura so that they become less visible to others on an energy level. On its own, Labradorite is known as an invisibility stone, however Red Garnet adds an extra boost of energy to strengthen the cloak created.

• If a person wishes to be **transparent** to the energies around them, then carrying Amethyst, Aquamarine, and Danburite together will help any lower vibrational energies to pass around and through them (i.e. they won't stick)

• If a person wishes to **reflect** any lower vibrational energies back to their source, just as a mirror reflects light, then carrying a Beryl and Bronzite together will help to reflect back any unhelpful energies when they reach the aura. Dowse to find the most appropriate Beryl to use - Aquamarine, Emerald, Morganite, Heliodor, Bixbite, or Golden Beryl.

• If a person wishes to be **dissolve** any lower vibrational energies which touch their aura, then carrying Lepidolite and Rose Quartz together will help dissolve these energies before they can become disruptive.

However, what must be remembered when using these Crystal Nets, although effective in the short-term, in the middle to long-term, any attempt to hide behind them and avoid the issues which are being raised by a specific relationship / situation will fail, as the Nets will have been used to avoid personal growth.

The best way to use these Nets is to allow someone to step back from a relationship or situation for a time, allow them to re-group and rebalance their own energies, so they can start to work on the issues underlying the relationship / situation, and so bring about real change. Once the Net is in place, it may also be useful / appropriate to place other crystals / stones within the Net for a specific healing effect, especially when a cord needs to be cut or a hole in the aura needs to be sealed. Remember, these Nets can also be used even when there is no obvious outside controlling influence, because they can create a secure and comfortable space for you to enjoy – an inner sanctuary which a person can relax into.

With many of these Nets, it must be understood, that even though these energies will no longer be attached to the your aura, they will not have been 'transformed', and so will go on to have a negative impact somewhere in the world. However, karmically, this is the responsibility of the person / source which is sending out these energies, and not yours. Do not allow yourself to feel guilt about this fact, as your primary responsibility is for your own energy field and well-being. Remember, guilt is one of the ways which someone can use to get you to lower your defences, so you really need to learn to *put yourself first* in this regard.

However, if you also want to transform the now disconnected negative energies, you can place a large crystal cluster somewhere around the Net, with the intention that the negative energies pass into the crystal cluster. Dowse to find the best place for the crystal cluster on the outside of the Net, and also dowse to find out the best way of transforming the negative energy after it has been absorbed into the cluster (i.e. you may feel the desire to leave the quartz cluster in nature for a few days, or leave it overnight in a bowl of salt water).

It is best to use a crystal cluster, as all the crystals within the cluster work together to create a group energy which is more effective at dealing with and neutralising negative energy. A single crystal can be used instead of a crystal cluster if necessary, but it will need to be of a size and quality that can store and deal with the negative energy safely and easily. It is good practice for the practitioner on the outside of this Net to also check if they need any protection as well, to protect them from any energies which may rebound onto them.

Finally, if working with a client who believes they are under psychic attack, it is best to keep an open mind – in both directions – and also to be willing to admit that you might not be the best person to help them.

Often people who are unwilling to face something within themselves can *project their issue outwards*, and claim that the negativity is attacking them from without, instead of realising that the real source is to be found within themselves. If so, the practitioner must devise an appropriate strategy to deal with this situation, to help the client see themselves and the issue correctly.

However, if there is indeed some form of psychic attack going on, the practitioner must be clear and grounded in their own energy, so that they do not also get sucked into negative energy, and they must also remain clear and grounded so that they can hold a positive space for the client (otherwise, how will they be able to help them).

In addition, calling for outside help, if the negativity being dealt with is too strong, is no weakness on the part of the practitioner.

An excellent book about the more extreme forms of psychic attack, and the problems untrained energy therapists can get into, is David Ashworth's excellent *Dancing with the Devil as you channel the light*.

<u>Note</u>:

Further information on Crystal Nets can be found in Sue & Simon Lilly's book *Crystal Doorways*. However, they generally advise:

- *Always allow yourself plenty of space and time - never squeeze a Crystal Net in between other appointments.*

- *The maximum time to spend in a Net is 20 minutes, although don't worry if you accidentally go over this time. You may also find that your experience deepens every four to five minutes. There is a definite shift of energy, a sinking to a new level. So the natural finishing times are five, ten, fifteen and twenty minutes or thereabouts.*

• *It is a good idea not to enter a Net if you are very tired - you are more likely to fall asleep than experience anything. Unless, of course, your reason for entering a Net is either to fall asleep or to wake yourself up!*

• *Always take time to come round to everyday activity slowly. Ideally you should have twice the time you have been in the Net before you need to do anything focused. This will give the body time to integrate the energies it has experienced into its normal everyday functioning.*

• *If at any time you feel discomfort or anxiety whilst in the Net, quietly get up and find somewhere to relax until the sensations disappear. Re-enter the Net or end the session and remain relaxing for a while.*

• *Drinking a little pure water before and after each Crystal Net session can help both with the removal of toxicity often released and the integration of new information and experience.*[1]

Each of the Nets has a particular coloured cloth as background (use white if you lack the required colour). This coloured cloth enhances the effects of the Net, but is optional, not essential. If you do not have a cloth of that colour, don't worry, the Net will still work as expected.

If you are having problems finding the crystals / stones for a particular Net, then a number of these Nets have been made into Audio Essences, Crystal Holograms, or Energy Cards. See the bi-annual *Samarpan Alchemy Newsletter & Catalogue* for more details (refer to Appendix D).

---

1 Sue & Simon Lilly, pages 15 to 17.

C14. Protection & Sanctuary Nets:

As discussed in the previous chapter, the following eight Protection & Sanctuary Nets each focus on a different protection strategy.

Shield Net:[1]

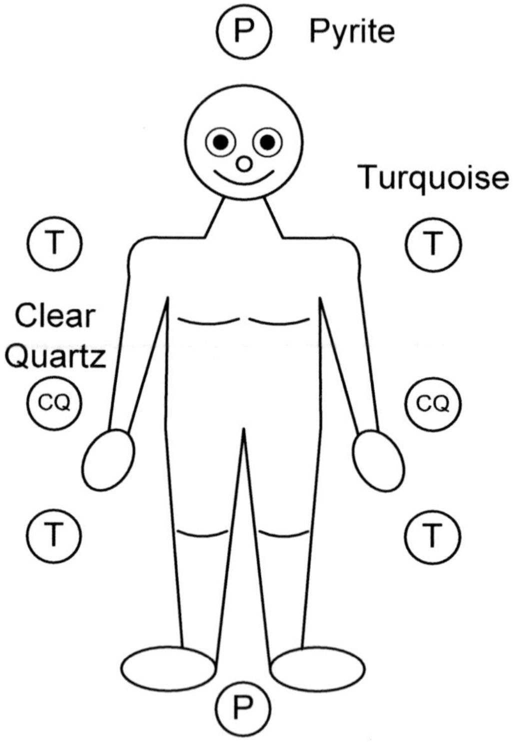

Figure 12: PSN Shield Net

1 This particular crystal combination originates from Dorothy Roeder's book *Crystal Co-Creators* (Light Technology Publishing), and was the first Protection and Sanctuary Net to be discovered.

Stones:

- 2 Pyrite cubes
- 2 Clear Quartz tumblies
- 4 Turquoise tumblies

Optional:

- White cloth as background

Placement:

- 1 Pyrite cube is placed above the head
- 1 Pyrite cube is placed below the feet
- 2 Clear Quartz tumblies (off the body) are placed on either side of the base chakra
- 2 Turquoise tumblies (off the body) are placed on either side of the heart chakra
- 2 Turquoise tumblies (off the body) are placed on either side of the knees

Use:

This Net works by *creating a shield* or strong boundary around an individual's aura, a shield through which invasive energies cannot penetrate while they are inside the Net.

This Net is also powerful enough to cut through cords and other energetic hooks, but only while the individual is inside the Net.

Unfortunately, unless steps have been taken to remove the cords and empower the individual, these cords will reform when they leave the Net. Fortunately, other techniques can be used to remove the cords while they are inside the Net without impacting upon its effectiveness. Dowse to find out what is required, although the chapter on *Dragon Points* will be a good place to start.

Anyone on the outside of this Net will also need to check if they require protection from any energies which may rebound on to them. There is a small risk that a cord or hook, that has become temporarilly severed by this Net, may try to attach itself to someone else on the outside. Although it will only be successful if this other person is relatively weak or unprotected. However, the good news is that, because this Net temporarily disconnects us from external sources of stress and anxiety, it can also provide us with a very empowering energy space, within which we can relax and re-charge.

<u>Invisibility Net</u>:

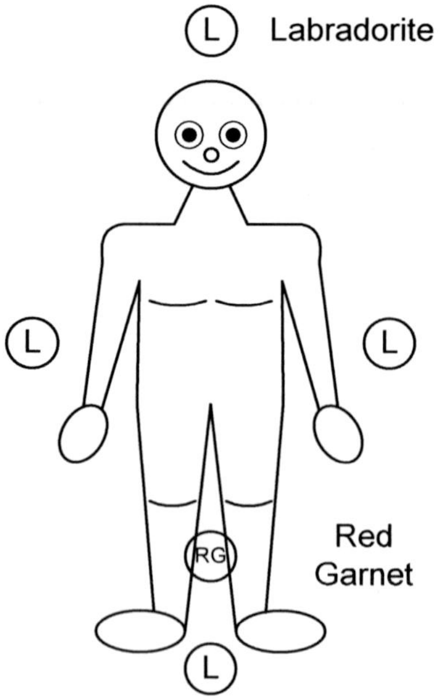

Figure 13: PSN Invisibility Net

Stones:

- 4 Labradorite tumblies
- 1 Red Garnet tumblie

Optional:

- Red cloth as background

Placement:

- 1 Labradrite tumblie is placed above the head
- 1 Labradorite tumblie is placed below the feet
- 2 Labradorite tumblies (off the body) are placed on either side of the solar plexus chakra
- 1 Red Garnet tumblie is placed between the knees

Use:

This Net works by making an individual's aura *invisible* to any external and invasive energy which is being projected towards them.

On its own, Labradorite is known as an invisibility stone, however Red Garnet adds an extra boost of energy to strengthen the cloak created.

While inside this Net, because the individuals aura will be invisible for the perspective of the invasive energies, the energies will have nothing to latch on to, and so they will be free from harm (while they remain inside).

However, remember, we only want to be invisible to invasive energy, and there are many situations in our life where visibility is a positive advantage, so it is not advisable to overdo this Net (i.e. we want to be invisible to the bad things, but visible to the good things in life).

Transparency Net:

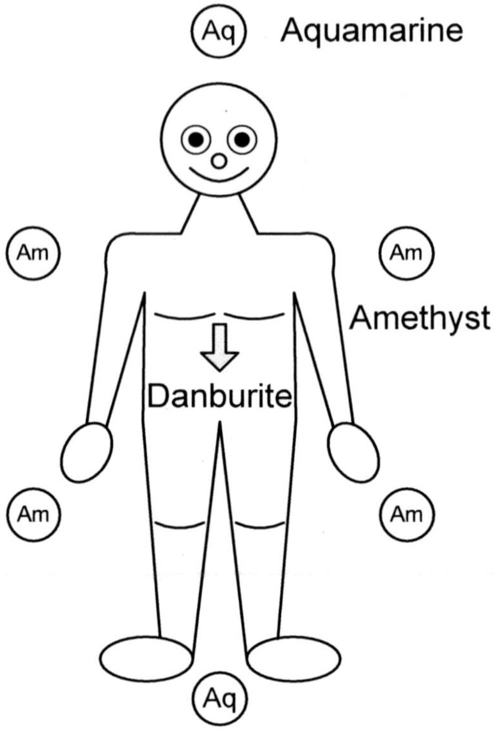

Figure 14: PSN Transparency Net

Stones:

- 2 Aquamarine tumblies
- 4 Amethyst tumblies
- 1 Clear Danburite crystal

Optional:

- Pink cloth as background

Placement:

- 1 Danburite crystal is placed on the solar plexus chakra (point upwards if there is one)
- 1 Aquamarine tumblie is placed above the head
- 1 Aquamarine tumblie is placed below the feet
- 2 Amethyst tumblies (off the body) are placed on either side of the throat chakra
- 2 Amethyst tumblies (off the body) are placed on either side of the knees

Use:

This Net works by making the individual's aura *transparent* to any invasive energy which is being projected towards them.

The Clear Danburite crystal on the solar plexus chakra, along with the Aquamarine and Amethyst tumblies surrounding the physical body, help to raise the vibration of their aura to such a degree that it becomes light filled and glass-like. Any invasive energy will simply pass through without connecting or attaching to the aura.

This Net also helps an individual to align with their own light body (i.e. the part of their aura which resides on the subtle / soul levels).

To work with this Net, therefore, for any length of time requires an individual to be comfortable with opening up to the higher levels of their being.

Transformation Net:

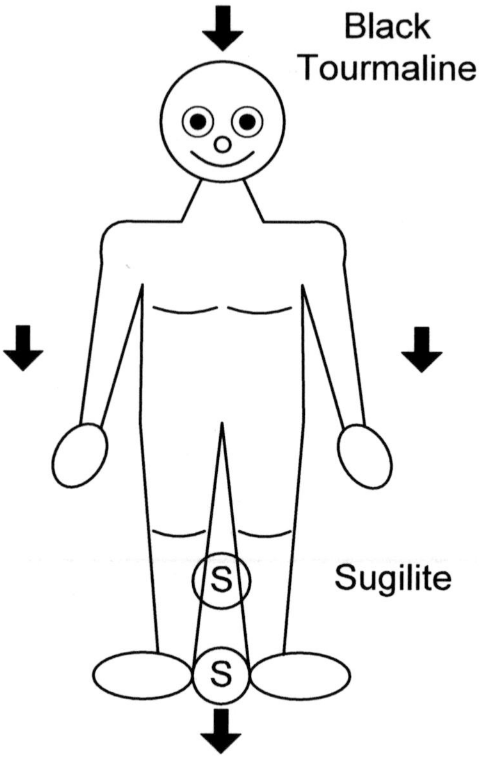

Figure 15: PSN Transformation Net

Stones:

- 4 Black Tourmaline crystals
- 2 Sugilite tumblies

Optional:

- Green cloth as background

Placement:

- 1 Black Tourmaline crystal is placed above the head
- 1 Black Tourmaline crystal is placed below the feet
- 2 Black Tourmaline crystals (off the body) are placed on either side of the solar plexus chakra
- 1 Sugilite tumblie is placed between the knees
- 1 Sugilite tumblie is placed between the feet

Use:

This Net works by *transforming* any invasive energy which is being projected towards the individual's aura.

The invasive energies are transformed into energies which are beneficial for that person, and which they can use in their own personal growth.

The striations of all the Black Tourmaline crystals are placed so they run parallel to the body's centre line, and if the Black Tourmaline crystals have terminations then they are all pointing downwards. However, it is also fine to use Black Tourmaline tumblies in place of points.

This Net will won't require a crystal cluster placed on the outside of the Net to capture and transform any negative energies.

Reflection Net:

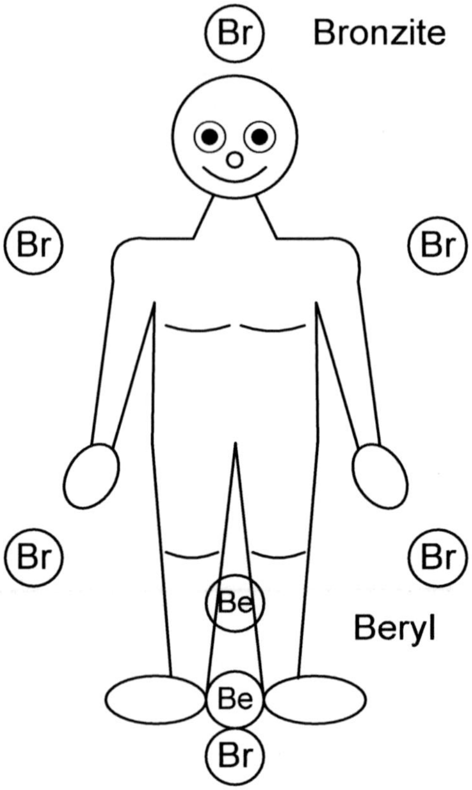

Figure 16: PSN Reflection Net

Stones:

- 2 Beryl tumblies
- 6 Bronzite tumblies

Optional:

- Green cloth as background

Placement:

- 1 Beryl tumblie is placed between the knees
- 1 Beryl tumblie is placed between the feet
- 1 Bronzite tumblie is placed above the head
- 1 Bronzite tumblie is placed approximately 10 cm below the feet
- 2 Bronzite tumblies (off the body) are placed off the body on either side of the throat chakra
- 2 Bronzite tumblies are placed outside of each of the knees

Use:

This Net works by *reflecting* any invasive energy which is being projected towards the individual's aura back to the person or source from which they originated.

It is important to understand that, while the person within the Net is safe and protected, the energies which are being reflected back have not been changed, transformed or transmuted in any way.

Therefore, if someone projects hate towards the individual, hate will be reflected back. If they project anger, anger will be reflected back. But if the source of the bad karma is not prepared to deal with their hate and anger, this process of reflection may only make the situation worse.

There are times when it is appropriate for people to send back the bad karma / energies they are receiving, but there are also times when it is better for the person on the receiving end to deal with and transform the energies (i.e. being bigger then the person sending the negativity, and taking responsibility for the situation even when the other will not).

You will therefore need to dowse out if this Net is appropriate for that situation, trusting that their Higher Self will understand the bigger picture and know the best action to take.

Even if appropriate, it is a good idea to dowse out how long this Net needs to be used. After this period, one of the other Nets may become more appropriate.

Any Beryl can be used – Aquamarine, Heliodor, Emerald, Morganite, or Bixbite – but each of the 2 Beryls must be the same type.

For the person inside, this Net can have an empowering, motivating and assertive effect.

<u>Dissolving Net</u>:

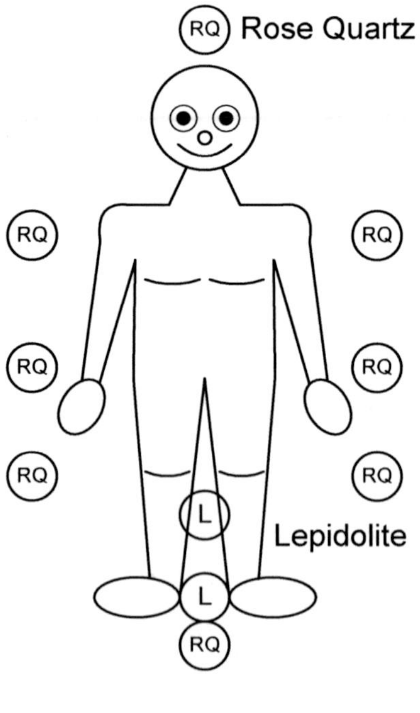

Figure 17: PSN Dissolving Net

Stones:

- 2 Lepidolite tumblies
- 8 Rose Quartz tumblies

Optional:

- Dark Blue cloth as background

Placement:

- 1 Lepidolite tumblie is placed between the knees
- 1 Lepidolite tumblie is placed between the feet
- 1 Rose Quartz tumblie is placed above the head
- 1 Rose Quartz tumblie is placed approximately 10 cm beneath the feet
- 2 Rose Quartz tumblies (off the body) are placed either side of the solar plexus chakra
- 2 Rose Quartz tumblies (off the body) are placed either side of the throat chakra
- 2 Rose Quartz tumblies (off theo body) are placed either side of the knees

Use:

This Net works by gently *dissolving* any invasive energy which is being projected towards the individual's aura.

While the individual is inside this Net, all invasive energies are dissolved back into their constituent elements, which are non-harmful and can be used in a more beneficial manner elsewhere.

The power source for this Net is the unconditional love and acceptance which is made manifest through the Rose Quartz and Lepidolite tumblies surrounding / on the client's body.

This Net may take longer to work then the other Nets outlined here, however, if the individual is able to persevere then it can be just as effective as the others, and this Net is definitely enjoyable and relaxing in its own right.

This Net will won't require a crystal cluster placed on the outside of the Net to capture and transform the negative energies.

<u>Coherence Net</u>:

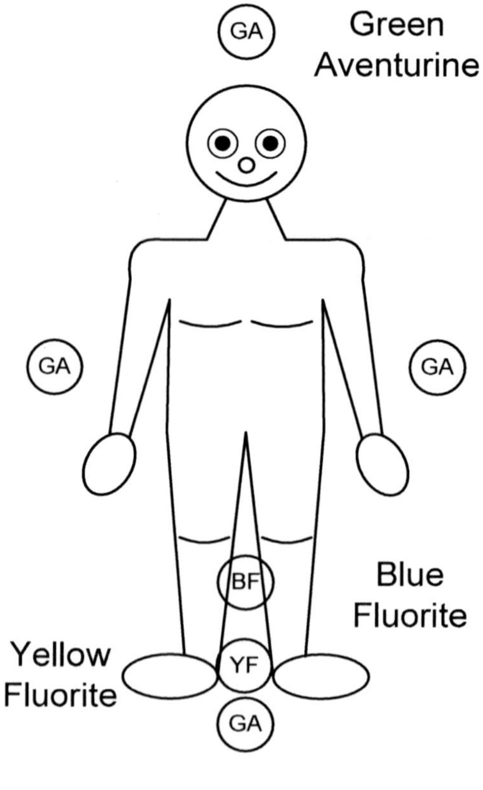

Figure 18: PSN Coherence Net

Stones:

- 1 Yellow Fluorite crystal,
- 1 Light Blue Fluorite crystal
- 4 Green Aventurine tumblies

Optional:

- Orange cloth as background

Placement:

- 1 Light Blue Fluorite crystal is placed between the knees
- 1 Yellow Fluorite crystal is placed between the feet
- 1 Green Aventurine tumblie is placed above the head
- 1 Green Aventurine tumblie is placed 10 cm below the feet
- 2 Green Aventurine tumblies (off the body) are placed either side of the solar plexus chakra

Use:

One of the reasons why some people drain energy from other people's auras is that they find it easier to gain the energy they need from an external source rather than undertake the discipline and inner work needed to develop the energy themselves.

As a result of this lack of self-responsibility and discipline, the energy of these people, energy vampires, is usually very disorganised and incoherent.

This Net works by surrounding the individual with an energy field of *coherence, structure and order.*

Basically, the Net reflects back to the person trying to drain / attack the client's aura the specific energies which they themselves require for their own personal development.

The person trying to drain / attack the aura is therefore given an opportunity to change, and they may indeed take advantage of the energy being offered to organise their lives for the better.

Unfortunately, these type of individuals usually do not want to change. However, this Net will make the individual's aura unappetising, and as a result these vampires will often go elsewhere for an easier meal.

The problem with this Net is that if the individual also has an issue with coherence, discipline and inner work, they may also find the energies of this Net challenging (which may be why they attracted their energy attacker to begin with).

Either Fluorite crystals or tumblies can be used interchangeably in this Net.

Perspective Net:

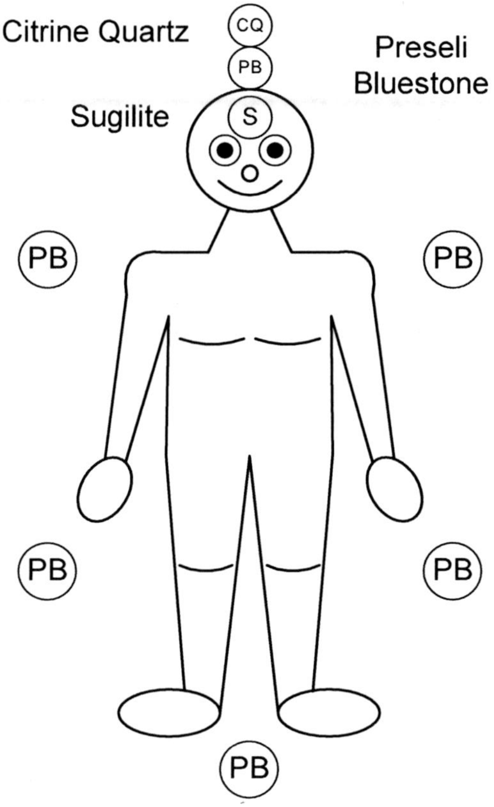

Figure 19: PSN Perspective Net

Stones:

- 1 Citrine tumblie
- 1 Sugilite tumblie
- 6 Preseli Blue tumblies

Optional:

- Green cloth as background

Placement:

- 1 Preseli Blue tumblie above head
- 1 Preseli Blue tumblie between / beneath feet
- 2 Preseli Blue tumblies (off the body) are placed either side of the throat chakra
- 2 Preseli Blue tumblies (off the body) are placed either side of the knees
- 1 Suglite tumblie on brow chakra
- 1 Citrine tumblie above the Preseli Blue tumblie at the crown

Use:

There is an Indian story of a man walking down a path at night, coming across a snake, and running away in fear, only to find, when he returns to the same spot in daylight, the snake was really a piece of rope left on the path.

Many of our attitudes and fears about a situation arise from the how we choose to view the situation, the perspective from which we have chosen to view the situation.

If we then choose to view the situation from a different perspective we may find that many of our beliefs are no longer valid, and our fears and reservations simply melt away.

This Net works by *opening the individual's mental body up to new thoughts, new perspectives and new ways of viewing the situation.*

Although this Net can be used with any situation where an individual wants new perspectives and insights, it is of particular use when people "feel" under attack.

Although it may not change the situation itself, it can help to change how they perceive the situation, which can take much of the pressure and tension out of how the individual responds to the situation.

The disadvantage with this Net is that the individual may have to be patient, as the new insights and perspectives may take a while to filter down to the conscious mind.

To help focus the energy of the net, a piece of paper defining the situation which the individual wants a new perspective about can be placed underneath the Citrine tumblie.

All of these Crystal Nets are also available as Audio Essences, Crystal Holograms and Energy Cards

C15. The Electromagnetic Reset Net:

Stones:

- 1 Lodestone
- 3 Sodalite tumblies
- 3 Red Jasper tumblies

Optional:

- Light Blue cloth as background

Placement:

- 1 Lodestone is placed on the solar plexus chakra
- 1 Sodalite tumblie is placed between the knees
- 1 Sodalite tumblie is placed between the feet
- 1 Sodalite tumblie is placed approximately 10 cm below the feet
- 1 Red Jasper tumblie is placed above the head
- 2 Red Jasper tumblies (off the body) are placed either side of the base chakra

Use:

Electromagnetic entrainment occurs whenever someone's own electromagnetic field starts to resonate at the same frequency as the electrical appliances around them.

This is possible because electrical appliances – computers, microwaves, ipods, televisions, and mobile phones etc. – have their own powerful electromagnetic fields, which use a higher and wider range of frequencies than the human body, and the weaker electromagnetic field of the human body starts to resonate at the same rate as these external E.M. sources.

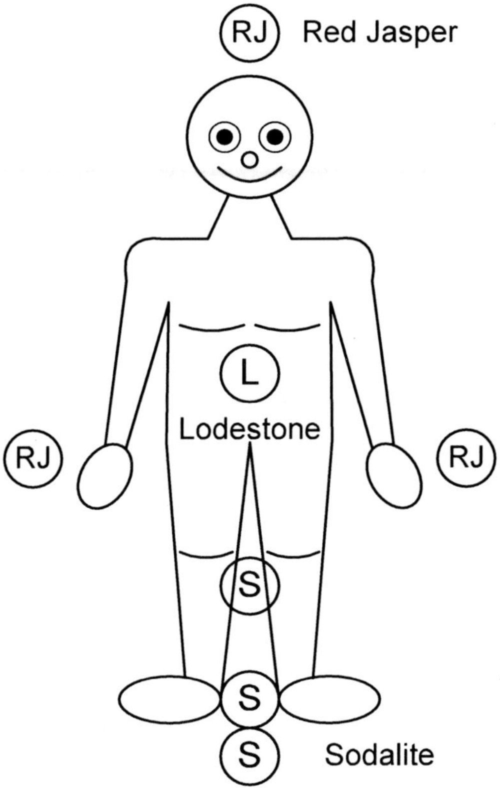

Figure 20: Electromagnetic Reset Net

This is a problem because all life on the planet has evolved over billions of years to use very weak electromagnetic fields to maintain health and well-being, and also these natural fields utilise only a small band of the electromagnetic spectrum available.

Conventional science now admits that the human body does create its own electro-magnetic field, but does not currently believe that this field is in any way connected with our health and well-being. They consider it to be just a by-product of living and with no obvious function or benefit.

I feel that Valerie V. Hunt's experiment with the E.M. cage, discussed in an earlier chapter, indicates the complete opposite.

But Nature doesn't usually develop something without there being a reason behind it, even if we can't tell what that reason is. Scientists used to say that the pineal gland had no functional use, or that the thymus gland had no function in adults. How wrong they were. A healthy human E.M. field is essential to our health overall.

Cars, trains and aeroplanes also emit an E.M. field, and when travelling in these vehicles a person is entirely surrounded by the vehicle's E.M. field. This is why someone can feel ungrounded after a long journey by car or plane, which can often contribute to the feeling of jetlag that occurs after such a journey.

When the human body's own natural E.M. field starts to resonate at a rate and strength beyond that which evolved to support our natural health and well-being, this puts the physical body under a level of unnecessary stress, which eventually takes its toll on our physical, emotional and mental health.

The human body naturally resonates on a frequency 4 to 7 Hz. The majority of electrical devices resonate on a frequency of 30 to 40 Hz. This is a potential difference of 23 to 36 Hz.

But why is this such a problem? Well... Just take a moment, and find the highest sound which your voice can achieve. Hitting this high note probably makes your voice sound quite squeaky. It probably also feels that your vocal chords are under some strain just trying to reach that high pitched sound (... OK, you can stop now).

Imagine if you could only communicate through talking in this high pitch voice. It wouldn't be long before your voice would start to crack underneath the strain, and you would develop a whole range of different throat complaints. Although you can hit the high notes if needed, your vocal chords are not designed to functional normally at this high pitch.

This gives you some idea of the effects on the physical body when it is required to operate and resonate above and beyond its natural E.M. range. It puts the body under tremendous stress and strain, which is not good for us on many different levels. And if the human E.M. field is indeed also being used for wellbeing and communication, the more stress it is placed under, the more these functions will be affected.

But why would the physical body alter its natural E.M. range? Well, if we return to our squeaky voice analogy. If everyone around you is talking in a high pitch voice then, eventually, you'll start to talk that way as well, even if it means you are also harming your voice in doing so. We are all programmed to fit in with the behaviour of other people and the world around us, it is part of our survival mechanism. And the same is true of our physical body and the E.M. fields which surround us.

The magnetic therapist Dr Sarah Brewer in her book *Healing with Magnetic Therapy* writes that:

> *Our cells' electrical activity has evolved within the Earth's static magnetic field, and it seems to be vital for health and for optimum immunity. We are also subjected to electromagnetic fields generated by thunderstorms in the equatorial zones. These produce natural, low-frequency (7.8Hz) vibrations in the atmosphere – known as Schumann resonances – that seem to have a vital stimulatory effect on our body cells, healing and growth.*
>
> *NASA has found that animals and humans will not survive in space unless their spacecraft are provided with a magnetic field similar to that of the Earth.*[1]

1 Dr Sarah Brewer, page 48.

The amount of E.M. stress that a person can deal with before it manifests as a physical condition / illness will vary from person to person, but as most of our modern society is now so totally dependent upon devices that emit an E.M. field in some way, it is very rare to find a person who has not been affected to some degree (even if they are not conscious of it).

In one of the companies where I used to work, they installed a wireless network throughout the whole building, as part of their 'embracing the 21st Century' drive. It was very interesting to see how different people responded to the increased levels of E.M. in the building. Some people reported experiencing disturbed sleep and an increase in headaches and migraines... while others reported no difference at all. Those who reported no change, and who were therefore probably less sensitive to E.M. fields or who had stronger constitutions, naturally concluded that the ones who had experienced a difference were just making it up.[2]

The phenomenon of people being hypnotised in front of their televisions, or becoming addicted to the use of computers and / or mobiles, is partially due to E.M. entrainment.

The most effective way to counteract this influence is to "remind" your body of the specific strength and range of E.M. frequencies that it needs to resonate with in order to maintain health and well-being. This Crystal Net helps the physical body to remember these natural frequencies, as the lodestone placed on the solar plexus chakra, vibrates at the same strength and frequency as the planet's own electromagnetic field (4 to 7 Hz).

While the client is inside the Net, all external, invasive electromagnetic

2 If science ever does confirm the existence of E.M. stress then the industrial compensation claims, from all those people who have suffered stress and illness at work, will be truly horrendous. This is probably one of the reasons why H.R. departments don't take such complaints seriously.

energy is blocked, and this allows the client's body to reset its own electromagnetic field. Basically, you are talking the body down from the unnatural range of 30 to 40 Hz, to the more healthy and natural 4 to 7 Hz.

The Red Jasper and Sodalite tumblies placed around the body help it to absorb and resonate with the natural E.M. frequency. The Sodalites placed between the knees, feet and below the feet also help to open up and strengthen a channel to our planet's own natural E.M. field.

If a person has been out of natural E.M. alignment for a while, it is not uncommon for them to feel discomfort / unease / strangeness during their initial exposure to this Net, but as their body remembers its own natural E.M. frequency, this is replaced by a sense of relaxation and deep physical ease, which can be quite enjoyable in its own right.

If a client is particularly susceptible to electromagnetic entrainment, or working in an environment with high levels of E.M. radiation, then it would be advisable to use this net on a regular basis.

It may be helpful to use this Net in conjunction with one of the other Protection and Sanctuary Nets, whenever you discover someone is under psychic influence / manipulation. E.M. stress means that their aura has been made weaker, leaving it open to various forms of psychic and geopathic energies, and so working on both issues simultaneously can strengthen the aura overall.

My ICGT students have nicknamed this the 'Turnaround Net', as after being in this Net, an individual often finds that their life seems to 'turnaround' quite dramatically, which may be an indication of how much electromagnetic stress distorts our natural energy field, which in turn holds us back. It is interesting that this is one of the Crystal Nets which comes up most often when I am doing a MBS fair or show, and people often report experiencing deep relaxation and ease, and a feeling that something has 'lifted'.

There are now a wide range of water essences, or other devices, to help protect against E.M. pollution. A search on the internet should find what is currently available in your part of the world.

However, just carrying a piece of Lodestone around in your pocket is a good way to remain E.M. neutral throughout the day.

Another crystal, which comes from Russia, and which helps an individual stabilise and ground their own natural electro-magnetic field is Shungite (which has become much more widely available in recent years). If you cannot locate a piece of Lodestone, then you can replace it in this layout by a piece of Shungite (although Lodestone is preferable).

Pacemakers & Alternative Layout:

Some people have understandable concerns about placing magnets, or magnetized stones, on a client who has been fitted with a 'pacemaker'.

Personally, I would also have concerns if I was using any high powered magnet, the kind which you often find being used in magnetic therapy.

However, a Lodestone has the same magnetic resonance as the earth itself and as the human body when it is in its natural state. So if the pacemaker was going to be damaged by the Lodestone then it would already have been damaged by the planet and the client's physical body, which are on the same frequency.

But if you or your client has any concerns about working with Lodestone, use Shungite instead of Lodestone in the previous layout, or use the alternative layout below, which does not use a Lodestone, but can also help to re-align and re-balance a person's E.M. field.

Electromagnetic Cleanse Layout:

1 Pyrite, 4 Lepidolite tumblies, 4 Black Tourmalines

Crystal Placement:

- 1 Black Tourmaline is placed above the head
- 2 Lepidolite tumblies are placed on either side of the throat chakra
- 2 Black Tourmaline are placed on either side of the base chakra
- 2 Lepidolite tumblies are placed on either side of the knees
- 1 Pyrite is placed between the knees
- 1 Black Tourmaline is placed between and below the feet

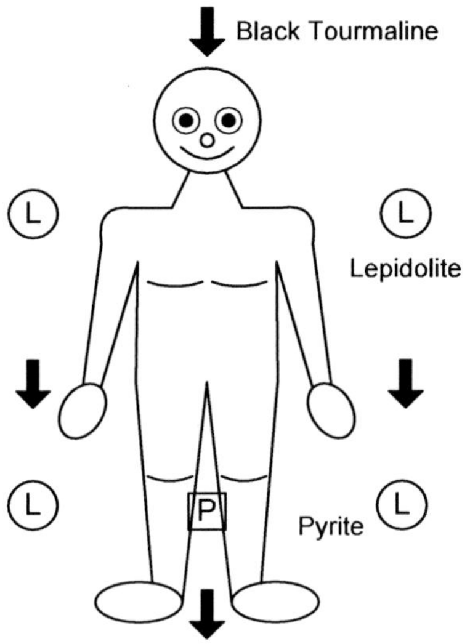

Figure 20: Alternative Electromagnetic Reset Net

If the Black Tourmalines have points, then the points are pointing downwards. None of the crystals are actually placed on the body.

Degaussing:

If your circumstances are quite limited, and it not possible to obtain any of the above items, then there is a simple but effective process called Degaussing which you can do instead.

Degaussing is a process which clears an individual's energy field of electro-magnetic entrainment.

Find an ordinary hair-dryer. The hole where the hot air comes out is at one end, and the electrical motor is at the other. Normally, you would point the end which produces the hot air towards your head. However, for degaussing you literally turn it around the other way, and point the end with the electric motor towards you.

You switch the hair-dryer on, and then you pass it through your aura, going from head to toe, over the entire surface of your body, moving the motor around in little circles as you go.

If you did have someone else available, then you could pair up and degauss each other. But if this is not possible, and you only have one pair of hands, then this is something that you can still do on yourself. OK, you might not be able to reach all of your body (i.e. there are parts of my upper back which I feel only a circus contortionist could ever reach), but you will be able to do enough of your body to make a difference.And, if possible, don't forget to degauss underneath each foot!

Degaussing is something which you can easily do on a regular basis to improve your electro-magnetic health and wellbeing. It helps to break up the E.M. entrainment which can occur between the human body and electrical equipment (i.e. the human body resonating at the wrong frequency). And one of the side-benefits of degaussing is that it also helps to ground you (win-win)!

C16. A Word from the Psychic Vampires:

Back in the 1960s and 70s, the popular image of a vampire was the actor Christopher Lee, dressed in a formal evening suit, white shirt, red sash, flowing black cloak, and long pointed fangs, who prowled the night in search of virgins.

Of course, they had to be young virgins, because 50 year old spinsters just wouldn't do, and they also had to be young *female* virgins, because young male virgins also wouldn't wet his appetite. Personally, I always thought blood is blood, no matter what the container it comes ready packed in. In contrast, Dracula was very fussy about his food. But it seems, back in the 60s and 70s, Dracula had the same desires and hang-ups as the young, heterosexual males who watched his movies. Strange that.

This stereotype was sent up in films such as *Love at First Bite* (1976) with George Hamilton, and also by Leslie Neilson in *Dracula: Dead and Loving It* (1995).

In recent times, however, thanks to TV series such as *Buffy the Vampire Slayer, True Blood, Vampire Diaries,* and *Being Human,* along with movies such as the *Twilight* series, and *Blade* trilogy, vampires have definitely received a make-over, and now are portrayed as being cool and sexy. The good ones go around, misunderstood, surrounded by a cloud of charismatic angst, desperately trying not to feed on humans, while the bad ones wouldn't be seen dead in a long flowing black cloak, but prefer dressing in designer labels. Nowadays, fictional vampires also aren't afraid to engage in occasional gay and lesbian 'feasting'.

But it is interesting that, just as fictional vampires have received a make-over, at the same time real-life psychic vampires have also decided to come out of the closet (or out from underneath the bed), and upgrade their own image.

This has been possible due to the internet's ability to connect people with diverging needs and desires. Before the internet, they would have been isolated and alone, surrounded by 'normal' society, afraid to go public about who and what they were, and what they craved. Now, they can connect over the internet, with other like-minded individuals, forming online communities to share information and provide ongoing, mutual support.

Now, I don't mean people who dress up as vampire Goths, or people who like to drink other people's blood as a turn on (yes, they do exist).

No, I am referring to people who openly admit to being psychic vampires. These are people who have a need to drain, or zap, other people's subtle energy to replenish their own. From their own accounts, these people consider themselves to be greatly misunderstood.

I first became aware of these people through reading *The Psychic Vampire Codex: A Manual of Magick and Energy Work* by Michelle Belanger, along with her other book *Psychic Energy Codex: Awakening Your Subtle Senses.* According to Michelle Belanger, there are some people who are born with depleted subtle energy reserves, and so have no other alternative but to occasionally feed upon the subtle energy reserves of other people in order to remain functional and healthy. Or at least, they claim to be 'born this way'.

The way in which Michelle Belanger describes it, when such a person zaps you, it is similar to when someone requires a blood transfusion, or when someone with kidney disease requires dialysis. Their body isn't functioning properly and the only way they can survive is through an occasional energy 'top-up'. Apparently, within this community there are many ethical psychic vampires, who only take from willing volunteers, or who never zap the same person twice, to fulfil their ongoing energy needs.

Now as a therapist, I have never knowingly worked with such a person, nor I have ever come across a person who consciously behaved in this way, so I cannot verify or deny whether there is indeed a fundamental weakness in their subtle energy anatomy.

But if it were true, then I would assume, framing the issue in terms of Chinese medicine, they probably lack sufficient pre-natal chi to power their mind-body system, and to also maintain and stabilise the rest of their post-natal energy. Without sufficient pre-natal chi, their post-natal chi would simply just slip away… like a planet without sufficient gravity to hold on to its atmosphere, where the atmosphere simply leaks into outer space.

But the point I want to make here is that there are other ways to get free subtle energy. It arises naturally from the fact that the universe is constantly expanding, and this means the fabric of space-time is being continually stretched (although I prefer 'massaged'), which in turn generates fresh prana / chi.

Believe it or not, our universe is generating free subtle energy all the time. The question is really whether you are aware of this fact, and whether you have the skills to tap into what is readily available all around you. And if there are other sources of free subtle energy available, then do you really need to zap other people to steal theirs? I mean, just imagine the icky karma it creates… let alone the guilt (conscious and subconscious).

The other area where psychic vampirism is sometimes considered 'acceptable' is when it occurs during sex. Within certain Tantric and Taoist sects there are meant to be practices were you can siphon off the core sexual energy of the person you are having sex with. This depletes them, and recharges you… but at their expense. This acquired energy can then be used to either re-vitalise your energy system, or directed towards your own spiritual enlightenment. The person who you are 'harvesting' can be in on the practice, or completely oblivious to what is going on.

Once again, someone could purport to be doing it 'ethically', where they never sleep with and deplete the same person twice, or downright unethically, where they continue to suck the life-force from a single sexual partner. But, from my own perspective, it seems like you're going to an awful lot of trouble to get something that is freely available if you know where to look.

During sex, two people are merging their energy bodies, so it becomes much harder to maintain an effective energy boundary. So if you are trying to hoover up their post or pre-natal chi for your own ends, how do you know that you're not also hovering up a lot of their other unprocessed debris... such as their anger, their guilt, their anxiety, their fear, and their depression?

On the spiritual path, sometimes something looks like a quick route to salvation / enlightenment, but when you look carefully, it comes with too high a price and many unforeseen consequences.

And, once again, just imagine the all icky karma it creates...

C17. Devices:

In the last 20 years, a vast array of 'devices' have come on to the market, all of which claim to protect an individual's energy field, and some also make the claim that they can protect homes, houses, offices and buildings. During this period, I have been able to trial a few of these devices. From my own experience, I feel that some of them work, do what they claim, are effective and value for money... and others, less so.

Unfortunately, it is beyond the scope of our book to list the pros and cons of the devices that are currently available. There are too many devices, and to undertake this task would require a book in its own right (and as soon as the book was complete, someone would bring out a new device, so the book would become out of date very soon).

However, what I can do is give you a list of questions I believe are important to ask when purchasing one of these devices, questions I believe can help you purchase the right one for you. Be aware, some of these devices can be expensive, and so it is important to be clear about what you require, what you are buying, and whether it will / can do the job for you.

Device Questions:

1) Some devices make the claim that they can protect an individual from psychic attack / influence, geopathic stress, or electromagnetic pollution. Some devices make the claim that they can protect an individual from two of these, while a few devices claim that they can protect from all three at the same time (and these tend to be the more expensive ones). So before purchasing, you need to clear about what it is you want protection from – psychic influence, geopathic stress, electromagnetic pollution, or all of the above. Once you have defined this, ensure that the device you are thinking about

purchasing is designed to specifically do this. There is no point in buying a device for countering geopathic stress if what you really want is a device that will protect you from psychic influence (although I have found that strengthening your energy field against electromagnetic pollution will also naturally help you to counter the other two, although not directly).

2) If you purchase a television, take it home, plug it in, switch it on, and no picture appears on the screen, then you will soon realise that it isn't working, and you will take it back to the shop, demanding a replacement or refund. But with many of these devices, whether something is working or not, and whether it is of real benefit to you, is a much more subjective experience. So you need to be able to gauge how you feel on a good and bad day, without the device, so that you can compare your experience when using it, to see if you feel / believe there is a definite improvement.

3) We are all individuals, we are all different, and we often respond in different ways to the same set of circumstances. This is why pharmaceutical drugs come with a list of potential side-effects, which arose during the clinical trials, along with the likelihood of them occurring. However, no doctor can predict in advance which (if any) side effects a specific patient will experience if they were to take the drug... because we are all individuals. To a degree, the same is true for many of these devices. Some people will find that some devices work better than others, while some may not appear to work at all. So the question is, if the device doesn't work for you, is there a money back guarantee if you are not satisfied?

4) Some devices are meant to work through attuning themselves to your own core energy. Once attuned, they cannot be re-used by anyone else, nor can the manufacturer sell them on again if you decide to return them (... well, they won't if they are ethical). However, other devices do not work in this way, and so can be

used by anyone, at any time, and shared between people. So you need to be clear about whether the device will specifically attune to your own energy or not, and whether you can return it to the manufacturer if you feel that it is not working for you.

5) How long will the device last, how long will it stay effective? Some devices claim that they will remain effective for an indefinite period, and will never wear out, while other devices are meant to have a limited life-span, after which they will no longer be effective, and so you will need to purchase a new one if you continue to need the protection.

6) Does the device require any ongoing maintenance, and if so, what is required, and how often? If the device requires regular cleansing to remain effective, then is this something you can easily and practically do? For example, if the device needs to be cleansed in sea-water, and you live 200 miles from the coast, then this is not a practical option. You may be able to use natural sea-salt, but then this is an ongoing and recurring cost you will need to consider. Some devices claim that they require no regular maintenance, and are self-cleansing... but then, how do they achieve this... and do you believe them?

7) Does the device need to be worn on a specific part of the body in order to work, or can you just slip it into any pocket and just forget about it?

8) Are the manufacturers upfront about how the devices are meant to work, and do they provide any research / information to back up their claims? OK, this research probably won't appease the scientific 'sceptic' community, but do you feel that it makes the device sound credible? Remember, if you believe in your device then the placebo effect, and its positive influence, will be working for you and not against you.

C18. Evoking Divine Energies for Protection:

One approach which some people use to protect themselves is to invoke the protection of divine / spiritual entities. They call upon the protection of their guide, guardian, power animal, spiritual teacher, enlightened guru, angel, archangel, or even God himself / herself.

Now, I am not against this approach, and if it works for you, then that's fine, go for it. As Gautama the Buddha once said, 'Truth is that which works'. But there are a few things to consider – the pros and cons – when attempting to use this approach:

1. Feeling that you are under the protection of a spiritual being really comes down to a matter of faith and belief. If you truly believe that it will work, then it probably will. However, if your belief is weak or non-existent, then it probably won't, and your lack of positive results will cause you to disbelieve even more.

2. No one, not even an archangel or enlightened master, can over-ride your free will. This is one of the *big* rules of our universe. So if you have chosen to learn a painful life lesson, then these beings are not allowed to interfere with your decision. They can help with the issue... but they are not permitted to remove the issue entirely.

Perhaps an analogy will make this point clearer for us.

Little Tommy is 9, and not very good at mathematics. He's good at lots of other school subject, it's just that maths isn't one of them. Each night he struggles with the maths homework he has been given to submit the following morning. As his parent, you love him, and it is agony to watch him struggle each evening, trying to complete this task. So you have a choice. You can either: a) help your son by spending extra time with him, gently coaching him with his maths homework, so that he eventually starts to understand, or b) help your son by doing the homework for him, so that he can hand it in the next day and be rewarded with an A+. Now, let's assume that at the end of the term, there is a formal mathematics test, which Tommy can't avoid. If you choose to coach and mentor him, then when he sits down to take the test, he will have all the skills and confidence to pass. But if you have been doing the homework for him, then poor Tommy will have no chance of passing, and you can't come into the classroom to take the test for him... So he will fail, and all his previous A+ scores will be shown to have been faked, and he will probably be devastated.

Now, the same holds true when we invoke the help and protection of spiritual beings, who can help, but are not allowed to take the final test for us. When calling upon spiritual beings are you asking them to: a) sort everything out for you so you can avoid learning your life lesson, or b) asking them to help you so that you have a greater chance of learning your life lesson, and so can eventually stand on your own two feet?

The two approaches are very different.

As you can no doubt tell from the tale of little Tommy, the best approach is b). We're here to do our own homework, and although we can ask for spiritual help and assistance, even for protection if required, we should never use it as a way of avoiding the life lessons that *only we can learn.* Attempting to do so is never a long-term solution... because there is always a test that only we can sit... so when it comes around, we need to have gained all the skills and confidence required to pass successfully.

3. You often hear people say 'I needed a car parking space... so I requested the archangel Michael to magic me up a free car parking space in the centre of town'. But do they really believe that using an archangel to find them a car parking space is the

best application of this powerful, spiritual being? It's a bit like me ringing the current Prime Minister of the United Kingdom, and asking him if he wouldn't mind arranging to take my car in for its MOT next Tuesday. There is a hierarchy of spiritual beings, and just invoking the highest one you can think of, to help you with some small matter, may not be your best course of action.

The same is true when it comes to spiritual protection, and the phrase 'using a sledgehammer to crack a nut' comes to mind. There are some spiritual beings that can be used to protect you from a psychic assailant, but there are others that are so powerful that they will literally blow that assailant off the planet... which may not be your desired intention. Remember, even though you didn't pull the trigger, it was you who called in the spiritual cavalry, and so you will have to deal with any karmic repercussions from this incident.

Your ego may like the idea of calling the biggest and the best entity available, but doing so always comes with consequences down the line. So you need to think about what is best for *your* situation. Do you need a traffic warden, or Arnold Schwarzenegger? If you are dealing with a parking problem, then getting Arnold Schwarzenegger around to sort it out, blowing up a few cars with his rocket launcher in the process, may not give you the outcome you want. Traffic wardens do have their uses.

C19. Unconditional Love & Forgiveness:

It may be odd to include a section on unconditional love and forgiveness in a book about personal boundaries and energy manipulation, but they are connected, very much so, and in several different ways.

There are some people who refuse to forgive their attacker, and who believe that to forgive would also be an act of condoning what happened. As a result, they are often stuck in the past, holding on to their grievances and re-living the events as if it were yesterday. For them, to let-go of the painful past, and forgive, would be an act of surrender, and they are not prepared to do this.

To be honest, there are also people who only suffer a small sleight, take it personally and won't forgive... and for others, the sleight is all imagined. Because they are continually in a state of high alert, they often have rigid and inflexible personal boundaries (because they could be attacked again at any minute, or from any direction, and so need to be prepared).

At the other extreme, there are people who go through life continually trying to 'turn the other cheek' and try to forgive those throwing slings and arrows in their direction, both physically and psychically. Although attempting to walk a path of love, their acts of forgiveness never seem to get them anywhere, nothing in their life seems to ever improve, and they always seem to be under constant attack. To an unbiased observer, it all seems a bit shallow, their forgiveness seems a bit fake, something which they must do, but which they really haven't got the hang off. Usually, underneath the façade, they are very angry individuals... but their anger tends to be passive-aggressive.

Because they believe their ability to forgive will also protect them, they fail to erect strong or effective personal boundaries (which is one of the reasons why other people find it so easy to pick on them).

But isn't unconditional love and forgiveness a good thing? I mean Buddha, Jesus, St Francis of Assisi... all the enlightened masters seem to be on message about the need for unconditional love and forgiveness.

Well, let's look at it from the perspective of our subtle anatomy.

According to the kinesiologist, John Diamond in his book *Life-Energy and the Emotions: How to Release Your Hidden Power*, love and forgiveness is the positive quality for the Heart meridian (the negative quality being anger), and the ability to actively reach out with love and forgiveness is the positive quality for our Gallbladder meridian (the negative quality being rage).

So when we do not allow ourselves to forgive, then we're actually storing up anger and rage in our emotional system, which in turn means that our fight / flight / freeze mechanism is switched on, continually pumping out adrenaline and cortisol into our blood. This puts our physical bodies under constant stress, and if it continues for too long, our bodies eventually burn out through having to deal with all these unnecessary stress chemicals.

So anger and rage may be beneficial in the short-term (i.e. it helps you to protect / assert yourself, stand up for yourself, and fight if required). But in the medium to long-term, you don't want those emotions circulating around in your system if there is no longer a need for them. Basically, anger and rage have a 'use by date', and if you hold on to them past this date (which is usually *hours* after the anger provoking event occurred... not weeks, months or years), then the only person you are harming is yourself.

Which is the reason why love and forgiveness are so very important, because being able to access these feelings helps to switch off the anger and rage, helps to reset our Heart and Gallbladder meridians. This means love and forgiveness has a major and beneficial effect on our emotional and physical bodies.

Seriously, forgiveness is not about condoning the behaviour of the other person, somehow accepting that what happened was right or justified. It doesn't even require that you become friends, stay in contact, or occasionally invite them over for a barbecue.

True forgiveness is about choosing to let go of a painful past so that it no longer influences your present and future. It is about choosing to remove anger from your life, so that it can no longer wreck / control your physical body, life and relationships. It is about choosing to allow your love to flow, so that good things can flow into your life, and so replacing the bad and out-worn. If you really don't like using the 'F' word, then why not rephrase it into something like 'Letting go of my anger and rage towards *<insert name here>* so that I can positively move forward with my life'.

One of the most important discoveries made by *Neuro-Linguistic Programming* (or NLP), is that the past is not an 'unknown country, and they do things differently there'. The past is being continually re-created in each present moment in your physical body. So if your body is continually wracked by anger and rage, because of something that happened to you 20 years ago, then the question becomes 'Why are you continuing to re-create those same feelings of anger and rage in your body NOW'.

It is therefore not about journeying into the past to access long-forgotten memories, which when uncovered give you the magical insight that stops the anger and rage. Unfortunately, just because you can remember the painful memories fully and accurately, doesn't mean that the mechanism re-creating the emotional pain in your body in this moment will automatically switch off. We now know that the mind-body doesn't work that way.

It's a bit like trying to switch off a light bulb by trying to access your memories of originally screwing it in place. True, memory is required to turn off a light bulb... but it's the memory of where the light switch is located on the wall... along with the physical act of turning it off, all in the present moment, which works the magic.

Your subtle self-defence mechanism is continually re-creating the pain in the *present*, not the *past*, and so the instruction to switch off needs to come from the present moment, and not through accessing any past memory.

Unfortunately, human beings are so caught up in their own story, and a search for meaning, that we often overlook the obvious (i.e. 'the light switch... it's over there... can't you see it!')

Energetically, true love and forgiveness appear to be the Off switch for much of our emotional pain. But did you notice then that we used the words 'true love and forgiveness'?

If it is really going to work, then the love and forgiveness can't be fake, it has to be genuine. Put simply, to forgive correctly, you need to have something to forgive... Which may sound obvious, and it is, but not in the way you are probably thinking.

Let's say someone steals the last hospital parking space from you, after you have been patiently waiting for it for the last 20 minutes (it's happened to me). You feel the rush of anger... but you decide to forgive that person (after all they may be late for an important appointment with their consultant), and so you try to let go of your anger.

Let's re-run that scenario, but from the perspective of one of the 'love and light' brigade, whose forgiveness never seems to get them anywhere.

Someone steals the hospital parking space which they have been waiting for patiently for the last 20 minutes. They feel a small twinge of anger start to well up from within, but immediately they push it down and suppress it, because they know that anger is wrong... and they decide to forgive that person for stealing the parking place (after all they may be late for an important appointment).

Can you see the difference? The difference is in how the anger was handled.

In the first scenario, the anger was allowed to rise-up, and was felt and witnessed, before the forgiveness took place. In the second scenario, the anger was not allowed to rise-up, but was automatically pushed back down inside, and the forgiveness was a plaster stuck on top of it. Therefore the anger was never actually *felt*. In the first scenario the anger was felt, but in the second scenario the person avoided feeling their anger.

Now why would *feeling* our emotions be so important to the process of transforming them? Well, most people don't want to feel their emotions, because most of their emotions aren't pleasant or pleasurable.

John Ruskan writes in his book *Emotional Clearing* about the vital importance of allowing yourself to feel your feelings.

> *To become integrated and to grow, you must accept and experience your feelings, whatever they may be. If you have failed at something, and you are disappointed, you must accept and experience your disappointment. If you are angry about something, you must accept and experience your anger. If you are compulsive, you must accept and experience the compulsiveness. Note that I am not saying you should act on or be motivated by any of these emotions; I am just saying that you must not resist feeling the emotion.*[1]

In Chinese medicine, positive qualities, such as love and forgiveness,

1 John Ruskan, page 126.

arise when chi energy is flowing evenly through a meridian. However, when chi energy is not flowing, has become blocked, then negative qualities, such as anger and rage, will arise instead. Therefore, to experience health and wellbeing we need our chi energy to flow evenly through our meridians.

Now, let us return to our two scenarios, and explore what may also have been happening on the meridian level.

In the first scenario, the car driver felt the anger... which is the same as saying that he registers on some level that chi energy is no longer flowing through his Heart meridian. However, after allowing himself to experience his anger, he decides to forgive the other person, and so his unconscious mind sends the command to allow chi energy to flow through the Heart meridian once again. This starts the process of creating the actual feelings of love and forgiveness, and his thoughts and emotions become aligned.

However, in the second scenario, the car driver doesn't want to experience his anger, so never allows himself to feel it. He's probably given his unconscious mind the command to never allow feelings of anger and rage to impinge upon his consciousness. If he never feels anger and rage, then he can say that he is not an angry person. Mentally, he may decide to forgive the other person, but this is entirely a head exercise.

But most importantly for us, because he never allowed himself to feel his anger, his unconscious mind is not able to send the command to restart the flow of chi energy through the Heart meridian. It remains blocked, and the *real* feelings of love and forgiveness are *never* generated. So his head is thinking love and forgiveness, but his actual meridian is still producing anger and rage. There is no alignment. Their Head and Heart are out of synch.

Such a person will go through life, speaking about love, but radiating anger... and they can't understand why they also attract so much anger from other people. It's a bit like when your car engine breaks down. To fix it you have to lift the car bonnet in order to access the engine underneath. If you are not prepared to lift the bonnet of the car, because you don't want to get your hands dirty, you will never access the engine, and so you will never fix the fault. You need direct access to fix things.

Now, there is a little equation I was once given, which I still find very useful whenever transforming limiting emotional patterns. The formula is:

- Feeling leads to Acceptance
- Acceptance leads to Ownership
- Ownership leads to Integration

In order to transform a limiting emotion you first have to allow yourself to **feel it**.

OK, initially you may not like the emotion, you may even hate it, it may make your physical body squirm, you may have developed many day-to-day strategies to completely avoid this emotion... but to have any hope at transforming it, you must first allow yourself to feel it.

If you won't allow yourself to even feel it, then you will remain stuck with this emotion. It's as simple as that.

Although there is a twist to this tale. It's not just about letting go of limiting emotions, but also about the thoughts and beliefs we hold about those emotions. For example, if someone has a belief that 'anger is wrong' then this will prevent them from acknowledging and feeling their own anger, and so releasing it.

But if you can allow yourself to feel it, even if only for a little bit each day, after a while, you start to realise that this emotion is also a part of you, and so you stop trying to avoid it... you may still not like it, but you recognise that it is also part of your emotional nature, so you start to **accept** it a little... and then a little more over time.

Next, a point comes when you start to realise that this emotion does have a place in your life, that it also has a positive side to it, and you start to really **own** this emotion. So if someone were to ask you 'Would you want to get rid of it?' your reply would be 'No, I think I'll keep it, it has its uses'.

Finally, a little way further down the line, you have **integrated** this emotion to such an extent that it no longer bothers you. In fact, it has become such a part of you that you no longer give it any thought. As Chung Tzu once said 'When the shoe fits... who thinks about their shoes?'

We started this chapter asking why include a section on unconditional love and forgiveness in a book about personal boundaries and energy manipulation?

Because some people try and use unconditional love and forgiveness as a way of transforming negative energies.

According to Tibetan teachings, if you want to create *compassion* you have to be in touch with your *passion*. If you are going to practice forgiveness, then you will need to have first transformed your own anger. But, hopefully, we have seen that for this approach to have any hope of working the unconditional love and forgiveness has to be **real**... it cannot be fake. And if you are faking it then this method won't protect you, and you are only storing up problems for yourself in the long-run.

All the spiritual masters - Buddha, Jesus, St Francis of Assisi - were able to love and forgive *themselves first*, and this is what gave them the strong inner foundation so they could love and forgive their fellow man. But people only see the acts of love and forgiveness which occur on the 'outside', and are unable to witness the acts of love and forgiveness which had to first occur within to make the external possible.

If that is your current situation, and you are able to be honest and admit it, then:

- Using one of the other boundary techniques may be more appropriate as a form of protection in your current situation.

- You may need to look deep within, and ask yourself why you are avoiding your own anger and pain. Read up about the Karpman Drama Triangle and see if any of it relates to you and your situation.

Energy Boundaries Volume 2 & 3:

If you enjoyed *Energy Boundaries* Volume 1 then you may be interested to know the subjects which I will be covering in depth in *Energy Boundaries* Volumes 2 & 3.

Volume 2:

Subjects covered in *Energy Boundaries* Volume 2 include:

- The Map of Consciousness
- The Placebo & Nocebo Effect
- Toxic Relationships
- How to protect yourself from Group Energies & Egregores
- Lightening Up Your Life
- Energy Boundary Nets
- Modern Psychology vs. Ancient Shamanism
- Invisibility & Self-Sabotage
- Positive Indifference & Positive Selfishness
- Glamours & the Pain Body
- Ancestral Healing & Thought Essence
- Chiron, Glamours & the No Boundary Space
- Past Lives & Soul Retrieval
- Absent Healing & Personal Protection
- Cook's Hook Ups

Volume 3:

This PDF is available to download for free from my website www.samarpan-alchemy.co.uk. Please see Appendix D for details on how to access and download.

It contains information which it was not possible to fit into either

Volume 1 or 2, due to space constraints, and so is being provided free to the readers of both these books.

Subjects covered in Volume 3 include:

- Meridian Gates
- Meridian Connections
- The Protective Power of Huna

In addition, the free bi-annual *Samarpan Alchemy Newsletter* contains an article about some aspect of energy healing, personal development, or personal protection

Each Newsletter is availble to download from my website on the 1st January and 1st July of each year.

Information about how to download the latest Newsletter please refer to the *Supporting Products & Newsletter* in Appendix D.

If You Have Enjoyed This Book:

If you have enjoyed reading this book, then why not take a moment to give it a favourable review on Amazon or other retail websites, explaining what you found most helpful and beneficial, and why you would recommend it to others.

Any positive feedback you can provide is much appreciated, and helps support small independent publishers, such as myself, who rely on positive feedback and recommendations to get our work out to the world.

And if you have found any of the information in this book helpful, highlighting it becomes your way of passing it on to other people in similar circumstances (which is what good friends and neighbours do).

In addition, why not befriend Samarpan Alchemy on Facebook, and leave a positive recommendation there, along with any successes you may have had using these processes and techniques.

Thank you & Best Wishes!

Brian D. Parsons
March 2015

Appendix A - ICGT & Me:

I trained as a crystal therapist with the Institute of Crystal & Gem Therapists in the mid 1990s, first obtaining my Certificate, and then later completing my Diploma in 1997. I have therefore been practising professionally for almost 30 years.

ICGT is run by Sue & Simon Lilly, who have published numerous books on crystal therapy and healing, including *The Illustrated Elements of Crystal Healing*, *Crystal Doorways*, *The Essential Crystal Handbook*, *Preseli Bluestone: Medicine Stone of the Ancestors*, and *The Crystal Decoder*, as well as many other books on personal development and energy healing. Information about Sue & Simon can be found on their website www.lilly-lilly.co.uk.

I started teaching ICGT Certificate & Diploma crystal courses in 2008, in addition to running courses based on information I have discovered and developed myself. I am also a Fellow of ICGT.

So the information contained in this book comes from two separate and distinct sources:

- Approximately 20% of the information in this book is taught on the ICGT Certificate & Diploma crystal therapy courses.

- Approximately 80% of the information in this book comes from my own personal research and development.

In order to be clear about the source of the information being provided, as you are reading this book, unless I state otherwise, it will have come from my own personal research and development. If the information does come directly from an ICGT course I will specifically declare this.

Now, after reading this book, anyone who would like to undertake the ICGT Certificate or Diploma training in Crystal Therapy can find out more information on the website www.mcscourses.co.uk.

The courses have been tailored to meet the individual needs of students, and currently the available options include a Foundation course, a 5 weekend course spread out over a 5 month period, a 5-Day Intensive course, or a Home study option. ICGT is also able to provide training courses for overseas students, and online study options are available.

In addition, I also offer training via my own school, Samarpan Alchemy (www.samarpan-alchemy.co.uk).

Appendix B - Crystal Perspective Training:

I currently offer modularised training courses based on the information and techniques contained within a range of Samarpan Alchemy books.

These courses are run via my school, *Samarpan Alchemy*, under the banner of *Crystal Perspectives Training*.

These courses are designed to help individuals:

- Change their perspective on life, and so change their life.
- Create strong and effective personal boundaries.
- Release thoughts, beliefs and emotions which no longer serve who they are *now*.
- Empower them with *new* thoughts, beliefs and emotions which are aligned to their ever evolving, unique personal path of growth.

I am deeply committed to providing students with a path of humour, commitment, integrity and trust. In return, I hope to attract students who are prepared to make a strong and serious commitment to their own personal growth.

If you have enjoyed any of my books, and feel that you want to take this work further and attend one of my *Crystal Perspective* courses, then I look forward to meeting you one day.

Please refer to the Diary page on my main website www.samarpan-alchemy.co.uk for information about the curent courses on offer.

Apendix C - Other Samarpan Alchemy Publications:

I have created Samapran Alchemy Publications as a way to offer readers new perspectives on energy healing and personal development, along with information which is practical, beneficial and inspiring. I offer a range of publications, in both print and ebooks, and the list of titles currently include (by author):

Brian D. Parsons:

Energy Boundaries: How to Protect & Affirm Your Personal Space, Volumes 1 & 2
Energy Astrology, Volumes 1 to 6
Grounding (What It Is, Why It's Important & How to Achieve It)
Really Useful Crystals, Volume 1
Crystal Antidotes: Harnessing the Power of Crystals to Resolve Personal Issues
Crystal Consciousness
Lucid Manifestation: How to Really Feel the Feeling of the Wish Fulfilled, Volume 1
Audio Essences & Crystal Holograms

Nathaniel Reeves:

Gay Polarity Tantra, Volume 1

Crystal Therapy Council:

How to Find the Right Crystal Therapy Course for You

More information about current and future publications can be found at my main website www.samarpan-achemy.co.uk, and also within the free bi-annual, downloadable Newsletter & Catalogue.

Supporting Products, Free Material & The Samarpan Alchemy Newsletter:

Supporting Products:

This book contains many practical techniques which you can use to ground and protect yourself, and so create effective, energetic personal boundaries.

This book is therefore not just about theory, although that does have its place in helping you to understand exactly what is going on beneath the surface, but aims to provide you with a range of practical tools and solutions which you can use to improve your life and current situation.

Many of these techniques do not require you to acquire anything, and rely instead on your own ability to visualise, or repeat an affirmation, or alter the dynamics of an existing relationship, or use the abilities of your own physical body.

However, the remainder of the techniques in this book do require you to acquire or purchase 'something'.

Obviously, this creates a few potential problems.

Firstly, your current financial circumstances may mean you are unable to afford a long list of crystals or other protection devices... even though you may be in dire need of them.

Secondly, for those methods which do require you to purchase crystals, although a writer can endeavour to show you techniques and layouts which use easily available crystals, unfortunately, this is not always possible, and so you may end up on a quest to track down something which is not only rare, but quite expensive (which is the fate of people who come under the spell of some crystal books I could mention).

This has always been one of my main concerns. It's all very well putting information out into the public domain, but I believe that this information must not only be practical, it has to be also accessible, easy to implement, and it has to be as affordable as I can make it.

I simply can't see the point in teaching people a technique and then saying, 'But it's all academic, because you're never going to be able to obtain / afford the materials needed to practice it for yourselves.'

This is why, in addition to physical crystals, I also offer three additional vibrational methods as ways to practically work with the techniques I will be showing you throughout this book. These three methods are:

- **Audio Essences**

Put simply, with an Audio Essence a positive vibration is converted into a digital sound file, usually an MP3 format, so that whenever you listen to that sound track you are also accessing the positive vibration which was originally 'recorded'... just through the act of listening. This is an Active method of working with these techniques.

- **Crystal Holograms**

Over the years, a number of different ways have been developed in which you can programme a distinct vibration into a crystal. The Crystal Hologram process, which I have developed, carries out the vibrational programming using a Light Life Ring™ and a laser.[1]

Using this method, the vibration which has been programmed into

---

1 A Light Life Ring™ is a wonderful piece of vibrational technology discovered by a man called Slim Spurling. You can read more about him and these rings in *Slim Spurling's Universe* by Cal Garrison.

the Clear Quartz crystal is very 'robust and stable', when compared to other types of crystal programming, and can only be disrupted or removed through a clearing process which also involves a Light Life Ring and *two* lasers. Also, each Crystal Hologram is individually created, and not mass produced in some kind of 'energy copier'.

The Crystal Hologram is a Passive method, and so works without your needing to consciously do anything. It is therefore ideal to wear whenever you need protection or additional support while going about your day-to-day life.

- **Energy Cards**

Just as it is possible to capture, record and store a subtle vibration on to a sound file, or into a quartz crystal, so it is also possible to record and store these vibrations on to a piece of paper or card. When you do this, you create an 'Energy Card'.

An Energy Card is a Passive method, and so works without your needing to consciously do anything. It is therefore ideal to wear whenever you need protection while going about your day-to-day life. They are cheaper than Crystal Holograms, and so may be more affordable, and unlike actual crystals, they do not require regular energy cleansing.

Note: More information about Audio Essences, Crystal Holograms and Energy Cards can be found in the free *Samarpan Alchemy Supplementary Manual.*

As a way to make these techniques as accessible as possible, not only am I putting all the information about these techniques out into the public domain, I am also giving you a range of different ways to work with them.

This is how I can fulfil my own criteria – to ensure that each technique I show you is practical, accessible, easy to implement, and affordable.

If you already have all the crystals necessary in your collection to work with a specific technique given in this book, great, go for it… and you don't need to obtain or purchase anything else. Just use them in the way outlined in the relevent chapter.

However, if you do not have the required crystals… but you do feel drawn to working with any technique which you feel is appropriate to your personal circumstances, then you have the option to work with that technique either via an Audio Essence, or a Crystal Hologram, or an Energy Card… and so you can choose the method which you feel is most appropriate for your own situation and personal circumstances.

In addition, on my websites I also offer a number of free Audio Essences to allow you to try them out for yourself, and so test their effectiveness before you decide to purchase.

If you want to know how to acquire or purchase any of these products, then at the end of this chapter you will find a section on how to access and download the *Samarpan Alchemy Newsletter & Product Catalogue* PDF containing all the products relating to this book, as well as my other publications. This catalogue is constantly being updated with new items, and has a new article twice a year (1st January and 1st July), and so you are welcome to download it as many times as you wish or need.

Free Material:

To accompany this book, there is also a range of free material for you to download and play with:

1) *Energy Boundaries*, Volume 3 - PDF

This contains a range of additional information about energy boundaries, some of which it was not possible to fit into either *Energy Boundaries* Volume 1 or Volume 2, but which I am now providing to my readers for free. To download this free PDF, go to http://samarpan-alchemy.co.uk/ebooks.php and enter your name and email address, along with the ebook code, which for this product is:

ZEUS9078

Once you click the Send button, the PDF will be automatically sent to your email account.

2) *Audio Essence - Optimism & Positivity - MP3*

This Audio Essence contains the vibrational signature for the Frequencies of Optimism and Positivity. To download this free MP3, go to http://samarpan-alchemy.co.uk/ebooks.php and enter your name and email address, along with the ebook code, which for this product is:

LITMUS1963

Once you click the Send button, the MP3 will be automatically sent to your email acount. This MP3 is 10 minutes in duration, and so should be OK to download into most email accounts.

3) *Samarpan Alchemy Supplementary Manual - PDF*

This ebook contains a range of supplementary information which will be useful to individuals new to vibrational healing, or who are just starting their journey of personal growth. It also contains additional information on Audio Essences, Crystal Holograms, and Energy Cards.

Because this information is useful to a number of different Samarpan Alchemy publications, it is has been placed into a seperate ebook, and is available to download for free from our website.

To download this free PDF, go to: http://samarpan-alchemy.co.uk/ebooks.php, enter your name and email address, along with the ebook code, which for this product is:

URBAN7698

Once you click the Send button, the PDF will be automatically sent to your email acount.

The Samarpan Alchemy Newsletter & Catalogue:

As stated earlier, this bi-annual newsletter / catalogue contains the current product list for Samarpan Alchemy, and is updated with a new article on the 1st January and 1st July of each year. It also contains:

- A new article relating to some aspect of energy healing or personal development.
- Our current book list, as well as information about future publications.
- Our current live course schedule for *Cystal Perspective* training.

This Newletter also contains our current distributuon websites and other outlets, so you can always work out which is the best place for you to purchase Samarpan Alchemy publications and products.

You are free to download this PDF as many times as you like, as well as distribute to your circle of friends.

To download this Newsletter PDF go to http://samarpan-alchemy.co.uk/ebooks.php and enter your name and email address, along with the ebook code, which for this newsletter will be the word NEWS plus the month / year in the following formatt MMYY.

For example, the code for the January 2021 newsletter will be:

NEWS0121

And the code for the July 2035 newsletter will be:

NEWS0735

Once you click the Send button, the PDF will be automatically sent to your email acount.

Important: If you accept to download any of these free products then you are also giving Samarpan Alchemy permission to use you email address for promotional purposes in the future... although Samarpan Alchemy will **not** share or sell on your email address to any third parties, and this information will be retained securely on our system. However, you always have the option to request that your email is removed from our lists at a later date.

Facebook & YouTube:

And finally, to keep up to date with the latest information, publications, products, releases, courses, and all other developments with Samarpan Alchemy, why not link up with our Facebook pages, **Samarpan Alchemy** and / or **Audio Essences**.

There is also a number of Audio Essences on **YouTube** which you may wish to listen to... so have fun!

About the Author:

Brian was drawn to his spiritual path from early childhood, enjoying his first experience of real meditation at the age of nine, and since then he has explored a number of different meditation and personal development systems. When teaching, he is therefore able to draw upon a wide and diverse knowledge base to help his students achieve their true potential.

He has extensive experience as an energy worker, and is a trained crystal therapist with the Institute of Crystal & Gem Therapists in the U.K. He is currently an I.C.G.T. Fellow, as well as one of their tutors and internal course moderators. He is qualified in Health Kinesiology, and over the years has studied a range of different therapies and energy systems.

Brian awakened his own light body, using the techniques created by Sanaya Roman and Duane Packer and their guides Orin and Daben, in the early 1990s, and has completed many of their graduate courses to develop and enhance his skills since then. To date, he has completed the LuminEssence courses which allow him to teach the following: *Awakening Your Light Body*, *Radiance (Self-Exciting and Filling in the Frequencies)*, and *Light Body Consciousness*. He is one of the few people in the U.K. authorised by LuminEssence Productions to teach other light body teachers.

Since the early 2000s, Brian has been developing his own series of Light Body Graduate courses, along with *Energy Astrology*, a personal development course unique to Samarpan Alchemy, and which allows an individual to directly experience the energies of their natal chart.

He is deeply committed to providing students with a path of humour, commitment, integrity and trust. In return, he hopes to attract students who are prepared to make a strong and serious commitment to their own personal growth.

Brian also has a number of formal qualifications in both business and teacher training, and so is able draw upon a wide range of experience in the 'external' world to help fuel his teaching and therapy practice. His formal qualifications include a B.A. (Hons), an M.A., an M.B.A (International), and a Diploma in Teaching and Lifelong Studies.

Here is what one of his former students has written about Brian:

> *Brian Parsons is quite genuinely one of the most inspired and inspiring teachers I have come across! As a student I found myself hanging on to his every word because each word was important, no word was wasted, each informed, encouraged and inspired. His thoroughness in preparation meant that each session was packed with information and totally supported with excellent paperwork. Brian teaches so that you understand, every piece of information is digestible, meaningful and if you don't understand the first time he will patiently explain until you do. His enthusiasm raises the vibration of the group so that wonderful and unexpected openings occur.*

Christine May

Brian can be contacted through his website www.samarpan-alchemy.co.uk. He currently lives in Devon.

Bibliography:

David Ashworth, *Dancing with the Devil: Survival for Healers and Therapists*, Crucible Publishers, 2001.

Dr Michael Bader, *Arousal: The Secret Logic of Sexual Fantasies*, Virgin Books, 2003.

Alice A. Bailey, *Glamour: A World Problem*, Lucis Press, 1971.

Michelle Belanger, *Psychic Vampire Codex: A Manual of Magick and Energy Work*, Red Wheel / Weiser, 2004.

Michelle Belanger, *Psychic Energy Codex: Awakening Your Subtle Senses*, Red Wheel / Weiser, 2007.

Paul Brunton, *A Search in Hidden India*, Merchant Books, 2014.

Paul Brunton, *The Secret Path*, Rider, 2003.

Paul Brunton, *A Search in Secret Egypt*, North Atlantic Books, 2015.

Paul Brunton, *A Hermit in the Himalayas*, Rider, 2003.

Robert B. Cialdini, *The Psychology of Influence and Persuasion*, Harper Business, 2007.

Mihaly Csikszentmihalyi, *Flow: The Psychology of Happiness*, Harper & Row, 1992.

Cyndi Dale, *Energetic Boundaries: How to Stay Protected and Connected in Work, Love and Life*, Sounds True Inc., 2011.

John Diamond, *Your Body Doesn't Lie: An Introduction to Behavioural Kinesiology*, Eden Grove Editions, 1979.

John Diamond, *Life-Energy & The Emotions: How to Release Your Inner Power*, Eden Grove Editions, 1985.

Gary Dolowich, *Archetypal Acupuncture: Healing with the Five Elements*, Jade Mountain Publishing, 2003.

Kevin Dutton, *Flipnosis: The Art of Split Second Persuasion*, Arrow Books, 2010.

Kevin Dutton, *The Wisdom of Psycopaths*, Arrow, 2013.

Dr Carol S. Dweck, *Mindset: How You Can Fulfil Your Potential*, Constable & Robinson Ltd., 2006.

Reinhold Ebertin, *The Combination of Stellar Influences*, American Federation of Astrologers Inc., 1972.

Cal Garrison, *Slim Spurling's Universe: The Light-Life Technology: Ancient Technology Rediscovered to Restore the Health of the Environment and Mankind*, IX-EL Publishing, 2004.

Liz Greene & Howard Sasportas, *Dynamics of the Unconscious: Seminars in Psychological Astrology*, Arkana / Penguin, 1988.

Judy Hall, *The Art of Psychic Protection*, Findhorn Press, 1996.

Judy Hall, *Good Vibrations: Psychic Protection, Energy Enhancement, Space Clearing*, Flying Horse Books, 2008.

Dr Sue Johnson, *The Love Secret: The revolutionary new science of romantic relationships*, Piatkus, 2014.

Todd Kashdan and Robert Biswas-Diener, *The Power of Negative Emotion: How Anger, Guilt and Self-Doubt are Essential to Success and Fulfilment*, Oneworld Publications, 2015.

Sue & Simon Lilly, *Crystal Doorways*, Capall Bann Publishers, 1997.

Sue & Simon Lilly, *The Crystal Doorways Companion*, Tree Seer, 2004.

Simon Lilly, *The Complete Illustrated Guide to Crystal Healing*, Element

Books, 2000.

Sue & Simon Lilly, *The Essential Crystal Handbook: All the Crystals You Will Ever Need for Health, Healing and Happiness*, Duncan Baird Publishers, 2006.

Sue & Simon Lilly, *Beyond Crystal Doorways*, Tree Seer Publications, 2007.

Sue Lilly, Simon Lilly, Brian Parsons, *Doorways in Time – A Workbook*, Tree Seer Publications, 2009.

Sue Lilly, *The Crystal Decoder*, Fair Winds Press, 2001.

Simon & Sue Lilly, *Preseli Bluestone: Healing Stones of the Ancestors*, Tree Seer Publications, 2011.

Bruce Lipton, *The Biology of Belief: Unleashing the Power of Consciousness,* Matter, and Miracles, Mountain of Love Productions, 2005.

Damo Mitchell, *The Four Dragons: Clearing the Meridians and Awakening the Spine in Nei Gong*, Singing Dragon, 2014.

Joseph Ostrom, Understanding Auras: *A contemporary overview of the human aura*, Aquarian Press, 1997.

Brian D. Parsons, *Subtle Anatomy & Energy Techniques (Samarpan Alchemy Supplement Book)*, Samarpan Alchemy Publications, 2015.

Brian Parsons, *Chakra & Meridian Antidotes: Harnessing the Power of Crystals to Resolve Personal Issues*, Samarpan Alchemy Publications, 2009.

Brian Parsons, *Vessel Antidotes: Working with the Eight Deep Fears*, Samarpan Alchemy Publications, 2009.

Brian Parsons, *Protection & Sanctuary Nets*, Samarpan Alchemy Publications, 2009.

Hazel Raven, *Crystal Healing: The Complete Practitioner's Guide*, Raven Publishing, 2000.

Havel Raven, *Heal Yourself with Crystals: Crystal medicine for body, emotions, and spirit*, Octopus Publishing, 2005.

Nathaniel Reeves' book *Gay Polarity Tantra Volume 1*, Samarpan Alchemy Publications, 2015.

Dorothy Roeder, *Crystal Co-Creators*, Light Technology Publishing, 1994.

Jon Rosnon, *The Men Who Stare At Goats*, Picador, 2012.

John Ruskan, *Emotional Clearing: Releasing negative feelings and awakening unconditional happiness*, Rider Books, 1993.

Alan Seale, *Intuitive Living: A Sacred Path*, Red Wheel / Weiser, 2001.

Suzanne Segal, *Collision with the Infinite: A Life Beyond the Personal Self*, New Age Books, 2009.

Martin Seligman, *Learned Optimism: How to Change Your Mind and Your Life*, Vintage Books, 2006.

Ben Sherwood, *The Survivor's Club: The Secrets and Science that could save your life*, Penguin Books, 2009.

Geoff Thompson, *The Art of Fighting Without Fighting*, Summersdale Publishers Ltd., 1998.

Index

Index

D

E

T

U

V

W

Y